Rick

POCKET

ITALY'S
CINQUE TERRE

Rick Steves

Contents

Introduction

Tucked between Genoa and Pisa, in a mountainous and seductive corner of the Italian Riviera, lies the Cinque Terre (CHINK-weh TAY-reh)—five villages carving a good life out of difficult terrain. With a traffic-free charm—a happy result of natural isolation—the Cinque Terre offers a rugged alternative to the glitzy Riviera resorts nearby.

Each village fills a ravine with a lazy hive of human activity. There isn't a Fiat or museum in sight—just sun, sea, sand (well, pebbles), wine, and pure, unadulterated Italy. Choose a home base according to just how cut off you'd like to be from the outer world: resorty Monterosso, cover-girl Vernazza, hilltop Corniglia, photogenic Manarola, or amiable Riomaggiore.

INTRODUCTION

The Cinque Terre

▲▲**Monterosso al Mare** Resorty, flat, and spread out along the coast, with a charming old town, a modern new town, and the Cinque Terre's best beaches, swimming, and nightlife. It has the most restaurants and the most comfortable hotels. See page 31.

▲▲▲**Vernazza** The region's gem—the most touristy and dramatic—crowned with a ruined castle above and a lively harborfront cradling a natural harbor below. See page 53.

▲**Corniglia** Quiet hilltop village known for cooler temperatures (it's the only one without a harbor), fewer tourists, and a tradition of fine wines. See page 81.

▲▲**Manarola** Mellow, hiking-focused waterfront village wrapped in vineyards and dotted with a picturesque mix of shops and cliff-climbing houses. See page 89.

▲▲**Riomaggiore** The most workaday of the five villages, with nightlife, too. See page 103.

Near the Cinque Terre

▲**Levanto** Town popular with surfers and families for its long beach; has speedy trains to the Cinque Terre, and offers an easy, level hike (or bike ride) to the sleepy villages of Bonassola and Framura. See page 119.

▲**Sestri Levante** Charming town on a peninsula flanked by two crescent beaches. See page 131.

▲▲**Santa Margherita Ligure** Easygoing old-school resort town with just enough urban bustle, a handful of sights, and close proximity to Portofino. See page 136.

▲**Portofino** Yacht-harbor resort with grand scenery and easy connections (by boat, bus, or on foot) from Santa Margherita Ligure. See page 149.

▲▲**Porto Venere** Enchanting seafront village perfect for a scenic day trip (by boat or bus). See page 155.

La Spezia Beachless transportation hub, with trains and boats to the Cinque Terre and buses and boats to Porto Venere. See page 159.

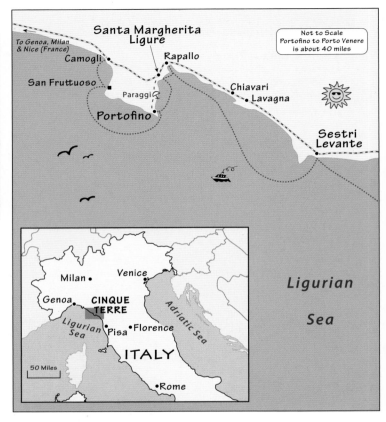

Planning Your Time

The ideal stay in the Cinque Terre is two or three full days; my recommended minimum stay is two nights and an uninterrupted day.

The villages are connected by trains, boats, and trails. There's no checklist of sights or experiences—just a hike, the towns themselves, and your fondest vacation desires. Read this chapter in advance to

Cinque Terre Area Public Transport

Framura
Bonassola
Levanto
Colle di Gritta
Soviore
Reggio
San Bernardino
Vernazza
Corniglia (Town)
Corniglia (Station)
Monterosso
Volastra
Manarola
Riomaggiore
La Spezia
To Carrara, Lucca & Pisa
Lerici
Montenero
Gulf of Poets
Porto Venere
Palmaria

5 Kilometers
5 Miles

CINQUE TERRE

See detail maps for
Cinque Terre
that show trail network

piece together your best visit, mixing hiking, swimming, trains, and boat rides.

Cinque Terre in Two Days: You could spend one day hiking between towns (taking a boat or train part of the way, or as the return trip). Spend a second day visiting any towns you've yet to see, comparing main streets, beaches, and focaccia.

Here's a sample day: If you're based in Monterosso, take a

morning train to Corniglia, hike to Vernazza for lunch (where you could explore the town, hike to the grand-view cemetery, or cool off at the beach), then catch the boat back to Monterosso to stroll the beach promenade. And that's only one day out of dozens of memorable Cinque Terre combinations you can dream up.

On any evening, linger over dinner, enjoy live music at a low-key club (or summer opera in Vernazza), try a wine tasting, or follow one of my self-guided town walks. At sunset, take a glass of your favorite beverage out to the breakwater to watch the sun slip into the Mediterranean.

With More Time: You may be tempted to add the nearby coastal resort towns of Levanto, Sestri Levante, Santa Margherita Ligure, and Portofino (to the north), and Porto Venere (to the south, anchored by the major transit hub of La Spezia). If you carve out a day and an overnight for Santa Margherita Ligure, you can fit in an afternoon side trip to Portofino. A day trip to Levanto (by train or a hike from Monterosso) with an excursion to Bonassola and Framura is fun. For double the beaches, visit Sestri Levante. South of the Cinque Terre, lovely Porto Venere merits a day trip.

Day-Tripping to the Cinque Terre: Speed demons could store their baggage, take a hike in the morning, have a waterfront lunch, laze on a beach in the afternoon, and leave by evening to somewhere back in the real world. But be warned: The Cinque Terre is inundated with cruise-ship groups doing the same thing. The best way to enjoy the Cinque Terre is to be here before and after the daily day-trip deluge. (Ironically, some travelers decide against an overnight because they've heard the Cinque Terre is crowded—then day-trip in, only experiencing it with those terrible crowds.) The charm of the region survives—early and late.

When to Go

In early spring, from mid-March through April, the Cinque Terre is typically all yours. Later spring and fall are peak season, with the best weather and the most crowds. Book rooms ahead during the busiest times: holidays (including Easter weekend and April 25—Liberation Day), May, June, all summer weekends, September, and October.

July and August are hotter and generally a bit less crowded. The winter is really dead—most hotels and some restaurants close from November to mid-March.

Before You Go

You'll have a smoother trip if you tackle a few things ahead of time. For more info on these topics, see the Practicalities chapter (and www.ricksteves.com, which has helpful travel tips and talks).

Make sure your travel documents are valid. If your passport is due to expire within six months of your ticketed date of return, you need to renew it. Allow up to six weeks to renew or get a passport (www.travel.state.gov). Beginning in 2021, you may also need to register with the European Travel Information and Authorization System (ETIAS). Check www.etiasvisa.com for the latest.

Arrange your transportation. Book your international flights. It's worth thinking about buying essential train tickets online in advance, getting a rail pass, renting a car, or booking cheap European flights. (You can wing it once you're there, but it may cost more.) Drivers: Consider bringing an International Driving Permit (sold at AAA offices in the US, www.aaa.com) along with your license.

Book rooms well in advance, especially if your trip falls during peak season or any major holidays or festivals.

Consider travel insurance. Compare the cost of the insurance

Make time in the Cinque Terre to wander, eat gelato, and simply be. Happy travels!

to the cost of your potential loss. Check whether your existing insurance (health, homeowners, or renters) covers you and your possessions overseas.

Call your bank. Alert your bank that you'll be using your debit and credit cards in Europe. Ask about transaction fees, and get the PIN number for your credit card. You don't need to bring euros for your trip; you can withdraw euros from cash machines in Europe.

Use your smartphone smartly. Sign up for an international service plan to reduce your costs, or rely on Wi-Fi in Europe instead. Download any useful apps you'll want on the road, such as maps, translators, transit schedules, and Rick Steves Audio Europe (see sidebar).

Pack light. You'll walk with your luggage more than you think. I travel for weeks with a single carry-on bag and a daypack. Use the packing checklist in the appendix as a guide.

The Cinque Terre

This breathtakingly scenic six-mile stretch of coast was first de-scribed in medieval times as the "five lands" *(cinque terre)*. Tiny com-munities grew up in the shadows of castles, which doubled as lookouts for pirate raids. As the threat of pirates faded, the villages prospered, catching fish and cultivating grapes. But until the advent of tour-ism in this generation, the towns—Monterosso, Vernazza, Corniglia, Manarola, and Riomaggiore—remained isolated. Even today, each village comes with its own traditions, a distinct dialect, and a proud heritage. Other Italians think of locals here as "mountain people by the sea."

ORIENTATION TO THE CINQUE TERRE

The Cinque Terre is now a national park (founded in 1999), where all can enjoy the villages, hiking, swimming, boat rides, and evening romance of one of God's great gifts to tourism. While the region is well-discovered and can get jam-packed, I've never seen happier, more relaxed tourists.

This chapter focuses on how to navigate the Cinque Terre, using a mix of trains, boats, and hikes. Chapters on each town follow, with all the specifics you need for your visit. For general advice on travel in Italy, see the Practicalities chapter.

Tourist and Park Information

Each town's train station has a Cinque Terre National Park information office, which generally also serves as an all-purpose town TI and gift shop. They can answer questions about trails (including conditions and closures), shuttle-bus schedules, and so on.

Useful Websites: The park's website is ParcoNazionale5terre.it. The "download" section of CinqueTerre.it has park info as well as boat and train timetables. A blog worth a look is CinqueTerreInsider.com, written by resident American expat Amy Inman; it's filled with up-to-date practicalities for visitors to this always-in-flux region.

Arrival in the Cinque Terre

By Train: The five towns of the Cinque Terre are on a milk-run line, with trains coming through about every 30 minutes; most trains connect to the Cinque Terre from La Spezia or Genoa (local train info tel. 0187-817-458, www.trenitalia.com). Big, fast trains usually speed right past the Cinque Terre, although a few IC trains connect Monterosso to Milan or Pisa.

Unless you're coming from another Cinque Terre town, you'll change trains at least once to reach Manarola, Corniglia, or Vernazza. From the south or east, you'll probably transfer at La Spezia's Centrale station. From the north, you'll transfer at Genoa's Piazza Principe station, Sestri Levante, Levanto, or Monterosso.

For details on riding the train between Cinque Terre towns, see "Getting Around the Cinque Terre," later in this section; for information on arrival in each town, see the "Arrival" section in each town

The Cinque Terre

To A-12 Autostrada
(Brugnato Exit)
SP-1

To Genoa
A-12

To
La Spezia
& Pisa

To A-12 Autostrada
(Carrodano Exit)
SP-566

To
Bonassola,
Sestri Levante,
Santa Margherita,
& Genoa
SP-370

2 Kilometers
2 Miles

Beverino

Pignone

SP-1

Pian di
Barca

SP-38

Levanto

To New Town
(Fegina)

To Monterosso's
Old Town

SP-1

SP-63

Monterosso
al Mare
SANDY
BEACH
Vernazza

To
La Spezia
& A-12

Punta
Mesco

Corniglia
SP-51

CORNIGLIA STATION
Volastra

Ligurian
Sea

Manarola
VIA
LITORANEA

To
La Spezia
& A-12

Riomaggiore
SP-370

To Porto Venere

chapter. For outbound trains, see "Monterosso Connections" on page 52 and "La Spezia Connections" on page 163.

By Train After Parking Your Car: Don't bring a car to the Cinque Terre; you won't need it. Given the narrow roads and parking headache, the only Cinque Terre town I'd drive to is Monterosso (and then only if my hotel had parking). Park your car in the nearest big city and take the train in—it's safer, cheaper, faster, and smarter. Parking is easy in Levanto or La Spezia (La Spezia has a fine modern underground garage at the station).

Helpful Hints

Pickpocket Alert: At peak times, the Cinque Terre can be notoriously crowded, and pickpockets (often female teens in groups of three or four, frequently dressed as tourists) aggressively and expertly work the most congested areas. Be on guard, especially in train stations, on platforms, and while you're on trains, particularly when getting on or off with a crush of people. Wear a money belt, and keep your things zipped up and buttoned down.

Money: You'll find ATMs and banks throughout the region. Use ATMs attached to actual banks. Shops earn a commission by hosting rip-off ATMs on their premises.

Markets: Market days perk up the Cinque Terre and nearby towns from around 8:00 to 13:00 on Tuesday in Vernazza, Wednesday in Levanto, Thursday in Monterosso, Friday in Santa Margherita Ligure, and Saturday in Sestri Levante.

Booking Services: Arbaspàa, based in Manarola, sets up wine tastings, cooking classes, fishing trips, and more (www.arbaspaa. com; see page 98). **Cinque Terre Riviera,** based in Vernazza, books rooms and apartments throughout the region, Vernazza opera tickets, cooking classes, and more (www.cinqueterre riviera.com; see page 55). **BeautifuLiguria,** run by Anna Merulla, offers various excursions (www.beautifuliguria.com).

Local Guides: These guides are knowledgeable, a delight to be with, and charge from €125/half-day and €210/day: **Andrea Bordigoni** (mobile 393-133-9409, bordigo@inwind.it) and **Marco Brizzi** (mobile 328-694-2847, marco_brizzi@yahoo.com).

Rainy Day Activities: Explore the towns, taking trains to connect them; splurge for a tasty meal; or nurse a coffee or drink at a harborfront café while watching the roiling waves. If you hike, avoid the steeper trails in the rain; rocks can be slippery.

Baggage Storage and Delivery: You can pay to store bags at or near the train stations in Monterosso, Vernazza, and Riomaggiore. Near the Cinque Terre, you can store bags in Santa Margherita Ligure and in La Spezia. To transfer luggage from the station to your accommodations, call ahead and arrange with **Roberto Pecunia;** he's based in Riomaggiore but works in any of the towns (mobile 370-375-7972).

Taxi: Cinqueterre Taxi covers all five towns (Matteo mobile 334-776-1946, Christian mobile 347-652-0837, www.cinqueterretaxi. com). The pricey **5 Terre Transfer** service is handy if you need to connect the five towns or beyond (Luciana mobile 339-130-1183, Marzio mobile 340-356-5268, www.5terretransfer.com).

Getting Around the Cinque Terre

Within the Cinque Terre, you can connect towns by train, boat, or foot. Trains are the cheapest, fastest, and most frequent option. But don't get stuck in a train rut: In calm weather, boats connect the towns nearly as frequently—and more scenically.

By Train

By train, the five towns are just a few minutes apart.

Tickets: A train ride between any two Cinque Terre towns costs €4. You must buy a new **individual ticket** for every train ride, and tickets are valid only on the day of purchase. You can buy tickets and check schedules online (www.trenitalia.com), at train-station windows or ticket machines, or at Cinque Terre park desks. When you buy a ticket, make a note of the train number, as that's how the station monitors identify incoming and departing trains. Don't wait to buy a ticket at the last minute: Ticket machines can be broken, and there can be very long lines at the window.

The €16 **Cinque Terre Treno Card** (described later, under "Hiking the Cinque Terre") can be worthwhile even if you don't hike, as it allows you to catch trains at the last minute without ticket concerns. It pays for itself if you take four rides in one day, but its value comes more from convenience than economy (https://card.parco nazionale5terre.it).

Trains are covered by the Eurail Pass, but it doesn't make sense to use up a valuable travel day here.

Using Tickets and Cards: Validate your ticket (or park card) before you board by stamping it in one of the green-and-white machines located on train platforms and in station passages. Conductors here are notorious for levying stiff fines on tourists riding with an unstamped ticket. (Train tickets bought online or with the Trenitalia app are validated—you don't need to stamp them.) Red-vested track-side staff can answer your train-related questions.

Schedules: In peak season, trains connecting the five towns generally run two to three times hourly in each direction, but the frequency declines after about 20:00. Note that some trains do not stop at all five towns. Check schedules in advance (shops, hotels, and restaurants often post the current schedule, and many hand out paper copies). Study the key to know which departures are only for weekdays, Sundays, and so on. These schedules also tell you which towns any given train will stop in. Trains from Levanto, Monterosso, Riomaggiore, or La Spezia sometimes skip lesser stations, so confirm that the train will stop at the town you need. (Train numbers starting with 21 or 24 generally stop at all five towns.)

At the Platform: Monitors display next departure times, listed by train number and final destination (but they do not show intermediate stops). They also show if a train is late—*in ritardo*—and by how many minutes; *SOPP* means "cancelled." Trains are indicated by their final destination: Northbound trains are going to Levanto, Genova, or Sestri Levante; southbound trains are headed for La Spezia. To be sure you get on the right train, know your train's number and final destination. Northbound trains use the tracks closest to the water; southbound trains use the tracks on the mountain side.

Getting Off: Know your stop. As the train leaves the town previous to the one where you want to get off, go to the door and get ready to slip out before the mobs flood in. Note that stations are small and trains are long—you might get off deep in a tunnel, especially in Vernazza and Riomaggiore (just head toward daylight). If train doors don't open automatically, open the door yourself: Push the green button, twist the black handle, or lift up the red one.

By Boat

From Easter through October, a daily boat service connects Monterosso, Vernazza, Manarola, Riomaggiore, Porto Venere, and beyond. Though they can be very crowded, these boats provide a scenic way to get from town to town (operated by 5 Terre-Golfo dei Poeti, tel. 0187-732-987, www.navigazionegolfodeipoeti.it).

Because the boats nose in and tourists have to disembark onto

Trains connect the towns.

Use a ticket machine to save time.

Swimming and Kayaking

Every coastal town has a beach—or at least a rocky place to **swim.** Monterosso has the Cinque Terre's biggest and sandiest beach, with umbrellas and beach-use fees (but any stretch of beach without umbrellas is free). Vernazza's main beach and new beach are tiny—better for sunning than swimming (some people swim in the deep water off the break-water). Manarola and Riomaggiore have the worst beaches (no sand), but Manarola offers the best deep-water swimming. Levanto, just a few minutes' train ride past Monterosso, has big and broad beaches, with even better ones an easy bike ride away, in Bonassola and Framura. And, Sestri Levante, farther north, has two beautiful beaches.

Pack your swim gear. Several beaches have showers. Don't tote your white hotel towels; most hotels will provide beach towels (sometimes for a fee). Underwater sightseeing is full of fish. Sea urchins line the rocks, and sometimes jellyfish wash up on the pebbles (water shoes and goggles sold in local shops). If no one is swimming, it's likely because of stinging jellyfish. Ask, *"Medusa?"*

You can rent **kayaks** or **boats** in Monterosso and Riomaggiore. While experienced boaters have a blast here, if you're not comfortable navigating a tippy kayak, this is not a good place to learn.

little more than a plank, even just a small chop can cancel some or all of the stops.

Tickets: Ticket prices depend on the length of the boat ride (€7 for a short hop; up to €18 for a five-town, one-way ticket with stops). An all-day Cinque Terre pass is €27; to add Porto Venere, it's €35, plus an extra €5 for an optional 40-minute scenic ride around three small

Crowd-Beating Tips

Italy's slice of traffic-free Riviera has been discovered, frustrating both locals and conscientious visitors. Groups—both day-tripping tours and cruise-ship sightseers—create the most dramatic influx. Avoid the worst of the logjams by following these tips:

Time your visit carefully. April can be ideal, with fewer crowds and cooler temperatures for hiking (although it can be too cold to swim). The busiest months are May, June, September, and October; July and August are slightly less crowded, but packed on weekends. Avoid holiday weekends (Easter and Italian Liberation Day on April 25) if you can.

Make the most of your time early and late. Take advantage of the cool, relaxed, and quiet morning and evening hours. Starting a hike at 8:00 or at 16:00 or 17:00 is a joy. Cruisers and day-trippers start pouring into the Cinque Terre around 10:00 and typically head out by 17:00. Those midday hours are your time to hit the beach, or find a hike away from the main trails. At midday, the main coastal trail is a hot human traffic jam. Beyond the busy coastal trail, there are plenty of hikes where you'll scarcely see another tourist.

Sleep in the Cinque Terre—not nearby. Levanto and La Spezia are close and well-connected by train, making them popular home bases. But it's easier to enjoy the Cinque Terre early and late—when it's quiet and cool—if you're sleeping here.

Be careful on crowded train platforms. At peak times, be cautious, stay well behind the yellow line, and be alert for pickpockets. Spread out to less crowded areas to wait.

islands near Porto Venere (2/day). Buy tickets at the little stands at each town's harbor.

Schedules: Boat schedules are posted online and at docks, harbor bars, Cinque Terre park offices, and hotels. Boats depart Monterosso about hourly (9:45-18:00), stopping at the Cinque Terre towns (except Corniglia, the hill town) and ending up about 90 minutes later in Porto Venere. Boats from Porto Venere to Monterosso run about 8:30-17:00. In high season, three boats per day depart from Levanto to Porto Venere.

Private Boats: To escape the crowds—or for a scenic splurge—hire a captain to ferry you between towns. For example, at the harbor

Hire your own boat. If regularly scheduled boats are jammed, consider hiring your own boat to zip you to the next town. Captains hang out at each town's harbor, offering one-way transfers to other towns, hour-long cruises, and more.

in Vernazza, you can pay around €50 to hop to any other Cinque Terre town. Split the cost among a few fellow travelers, and you have an affordable water taxi. Captains offer their services at the harbors in Monterosso, Vernazza, Manarola, and Riomaggiore (see specific listings in the Monterosso and Vernazza sections).

By Shuttle Bus

ATC shuttle buses (which locals call *pulmino*) connect each Cinque Terre town with its closest parking lot and various points in the hills (but they don't connect the five towns to each other). The one you're most likely to use runs between Corniglia's train station and its hilltop town center. Rides cost €1.50 (€2.50 from driver), and are covered by

Boats connect the towns.

Shuttles link to parking and hikes.

the Cinque Terre park card (described in next section). Buy tickets and get bus schedules at park info offices or TIs, or check times posted at bus stops (also online at www.atcesercizio.it). As you board, it's smart to tell the driver where you want to go. Departures often coordinate with train arrival times.

Some shuttles go beyond the parking lots and high into the hills—often terminating at the town's sanctuary church. To soak in the scenery, you can ride up and hike down. This works particularly well from Manarola and Vernazza. Or you can ride both ways (50 minutes round-trip, covered by one ticket).

HIKING THE CINQUE TERRE

The five Cinque Terre towns are connected by a main coastal trail and a web of trails higher up. The main coastal trail has four sections—two that are open (Monterosso to Vernazza, and Vernazza to Corniglia) and two that are closed (Corniglia to Manarola, and Manarola to Riomaggiore—the famed "Via dell'Amore"). Also closed is the alternate Riomaggiore-Manarola trail (via "La Beccara").

With only half the trails open and so many day-trippers blitzing in with the same hiking agenda, you'll want to enjoy the region's most popular hikes on the lower trail (from Vernazza to Monterosso, or from Corniglia to Vernazza) early or late. The single best high-country hike is from Manarola to Corniglia via Volastra. These hikes take roughly 1.5-2 hours and are described next.

Cinque Terre Park Card: Visitors hiking on the main coastal trail must buy a park card. Cards are not needed to hike on higher

Signs, markers, and arrows help guide hikers on the Cinque Terre's many trails.

trails. Cards can be purchased online, or at train stations, TIs, and trailheads, and are good for 24 or 48 hours after validation (www. parconazionale5terre.it). Some area hotels sell discounted park cards to guests—be sure to ask.

The **Cinque Terre Trekking Card** costs €7.50 for one day of hiking or €14.50 for two days (covers trails, free use of WCs, park Wi-Fi, and ATC shuttle buses, but not trains).

The **Cinque Terre Treno Card** covers what the Trekking Card does, but also includes local trains connecting all Cinque Terre towns, plus Levanto and La Spezia (€16/24 hours, €29/48 hours, validate card at train station by punching it in the machine). Even if you're not planning to hike, this card can be worth it just to save you time on buying train tickets.

Navigation: Trails are marked with red-and-white paint, white arrows, and some signs (*sentiero* means trail). The main coastal trail is variously indicated as "SVA," "the Blue Trail," or #592. Maps aren't necessary for the basic coastal hikes. But for the more challenging routes that leave the crowds behind, pick up a good hiking map (about €5, sold everywhere).

Hiking Conditions: In general, trails are narrow, steep, rocky, and come with lots of challenging steps. Don't overestimate your hiking abilities. I get many emails from readers who say the trails were tougher than they'd expected. The rocks and metal grates can be slippery in the rain. Don't venture up on these rocky cliffs without sun protection (and/or a hat), water, and proper shoes (flip-flops are not allowed). Pace yourself. While the main coastal trail is strenuous, it's doable for any fit hiker...and the scenery is worth the sweat.

Hikes at a Glance

Hikes can be done in either direction. Get local advice before you set out. I've omitted trails closed as of this printing.

Main Coastal Trail

▲▲▲**Vernazza-Monterosso** Challenging but dramatic 2-hour hike, including long stretches of steep steps above Monterosso.

▲▲▲**Corniglia-Vernazza** Most scenic and rewarding segment (1.5 hours) of the main coastal trail, with fine views, significant elevation changes, and moderately challenging stretches on uneven stone steps.

Above the Main Coastal Trail

▲▲**Manarola-Corniglia via Volastra** Demanding but gorgeous 2.5-hour hike through vineyards high over the coast; made much easier and shorter if you take the shuttle bus from Manarola to Volastra. Park card not required for hike, though it covers the cheap bus ride.

▲▲**Madonna di Reggio Sanctuary Hike** Easy 30-minute downhill hike from the sanctuary above Vernazza, best reached by shuttle bus. See page 67.

Extending the Coastal Trail and More

To the North

▲**Monterosso-Levanto** Logical northward continuation of the main coastal trail, a 3.5-hour hike over Punta Mesco; a notch more challenging and longer than other coastal trail segments.

▲**Levanto-Bonassola Promenade** Level 30-minute walk that cuts through mountains (largely through tunnels) to connect Levanto to the beach town of Bonassola; fine by foot but better by bike. See page 124.

▲**Bonassola-Framura** Level 30-minute walk from Bonassola through a

Before embarking on the more difficult hikes, get advice from one of the national park offices (located at each train station), or from Cinque Terre Trekking in Manarola (see page 97).

When to Go: The coastal trail can be extremely crowded and very hot at midday. For the best light, coolest temperatures, and fewer crowds, start your hike early (by 8:00) or late (around 16:00 or 17:00).

long line of train tunnels (better by bike) to Framura's train station; can continue to several small beaches (easy cliffside trail) or up to a cluster of little villages (via a footpath). See page 125.

To the South
▲ **Riomaggiore-Porto Venere** Very demanding 6-hour trek high into the hills, ending at picturesque Porto Venere.

Long, Cross-Regional Hike
▲ **High Route between Porto Venere and Levanto** Remote, cliff-capping 22-mile trail (AV5T) high above the main coastal trail and sanctuary trails; best for well-equipped, hardy hikers.

Before setting out for an evening hike, find out when the sun will set, and leave plenty of time to arrive at your destination before then; there's no lighting on the trails.

Shuttle Buses: ATC shuttle buses can make the going easier, connecting coastal villages to trailheads higher up. Locals know all the options—and shuttle bus schedules—so ask around. But be aware that

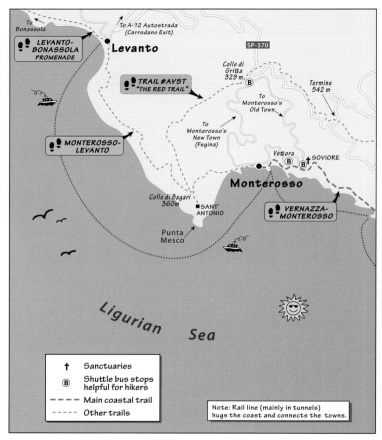

To Bonassola

To A-12 Autostrada
(Carrodano Exit)

SP-370

LEVANTO-
BONASSOLA
PROMENADE

Levanto

Colle di
Gritta
329 m.

Ⓑ

Termine
542 m

TRAIL #AV5T
"THE RED TRAIL"

To
Monterosso's
Old Town

MONTEROSSO-
LEVANTO

To
Monterosso's
New Town
(Fegina)

Vettora

Ⓑ

Ⓑ ✝ SOVIORE

Monterosso

Colle di Bagari
360m

■SANT'
ANTONIO

VERNAZZA-
MONTEROSSO

Punta
Mesco

Ligurian

Sea

✝	Sanctuaries
Ⓑ	Shuttle bus stops helpful for hikers
– – –	Main coastal trail
· · · ·	Other trails

Note: Rail line (mainly in tunnels)
hugs the coast and connects the towns.

shuttles heading into the high country only run in summer, and just once or twice a day. If frustrated with bus schedules, try the local taxis.

Guided Hikes and Excursions: Your park card includes guided hikes and other local excursions (such as town walking tours), which take place almost daily in the summer months. Even without a valid

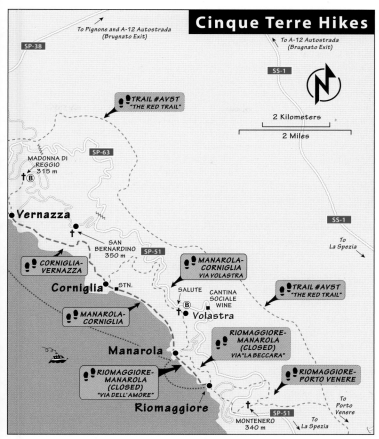

Cinque Terre Hikes

park ticket, these events are affordable—usually around €6. Look for schedules locally, or email visiteguidate@ati5terre.it for details.

Top Three Hikes

These three hikes each give the quintessential Cinque Terre hiking experience. The first two are part of the main coastal trail (and require the national park card); the third takes you much higher (and is free).

Main Coastal Trail

▲▲▲Vernazza-Monterosso (2 hours, 2 miles)

The scenic up-and-down-a-lot trek from Vernazza to Monterosso is both challenging and rewarding. The trail is narrow, steep, and crumbly in spots, with a lot of steps but easy to follow. The views just out of Vernazza, looking back at the town, are spectacular. From there you'll gradually ascend to 550 feet, passing some scenic waterfalls populated by croaking frogs. As you approach Monterosso, you'll descend steeply through vineyards—on very deep, knee-testing stairs—and eventually follow a rivulet to the sea. The last stretch is along a pleasant, paved pathway clinging to the cliff. You'll pop out right at Monterosso's refreshing old-town beach.

▲▲▲Corniglia-Vernazza (1.5 hours, 2 miles)

The hike from Corniglia to Vernazza—the wildest and greenest section of the coast—is very rewarding but very hilly. From the Corniglia train station, zigzag up to the town (via the steep stairs, the longer road, or the shuttle bus). From Corniglia, you'll reach the trailhead on the main road, past Villa Cecio. You'll hike through vineyards toward Vernazza. After about 10 minutes, you'll see a faded sign to Guvano beach, far beneath you (formerly a nude beach—now closed). The scenic trail continues through lots of fragrant and flowery vegetation into Vernazza. If you need a break before reaching Vernazza, stop at Bar la Torre, with a strip of amazingly scenic and delightfully shady tables perched high above the town.

Above the Main Coastal Trail

▲▲Manarola-Corniglia via Volastra (2.5 hours, 4 miles)

This challenging hike from Manarola leads up to the village of Volastra, then north through high-altitude vineyard terraces, and steeply down through a forest to Corniglia. You can shave the two steepest miles off this route by taking the ATC shuttle bus from Manarola up to Volastra (about hourly, 15-minute trip).

If you'd rather hike to Volastra, you have two options: The national park's official route (trail #506) cuts up through the valley. Locals have cleared a more scenic but rougher alternate route that begins

The high trail to Volastra offers breathtaking views.

with the vineyard hike on my self-guided walk for Manarola (page 91); partway along this walk, where you reach the wooden religious scenes scampering up the hillside, take a sharp right and walk uphill, following signs for *Panoramico Volastra (Corniglia)*. While steeper than the official route, this trail follows the ridge at the top of the vineyard, with wonderful sea views.

Tiny **Volastra,** perched between Manarola and Corniglia, hosts lots of Germans and Italians in the summer. Just below town, in the hamlet of Groppo, is Cantina Sociale, a cooperative winery open to the public (wine tastings, www.cantinacinqueterre.com). When you're ready to head for Corniglia, make your way to the village church (where the shuttle bus drops off) and look for *Corniglia* signs. From the front door of the church, directly across the piazza, find the trailhead (marked by an iron cross) for trail #586 to Case Pianca.

Here begins one of the region's finest hikes, tight-roping along narrow trails tucked between vineyard terraces, with spectacular bird's-eye views over the entire Cinque Terre. You'll cut up and down the terraces a bit—just keep following the red-and-white markings and arrows. After passing a little village (and following signs through someone's seaview backyard), the trail enters a forest and begins its sharp, rocky descent into Corniglia. (To skip the descent, backtrack to Volastra and return by shuttle bus to Manarola.) High above Corniglia, you'll reach a fork, where you turn left to proceed downhill on trail #587 to Corniglia.

Extending the Coastal Trail

Beyond the main coastal trail, the national park maintains a free, extensive network of trails. The Cinque Terre Park Card is not required for the following hikes.

The most challenging hikes (between Riomaggiore and Porto Venere, and the high route linking Porto Venere and Levanto) are best for very experienced hikers who are equipped with hiking boots, poles, a phone for emergencies, plenty of water, and a good map. Before attempting these hikes, get detailed local advice.

To the North

▲Monterosso-Levanto (3.5 hours, 4 miles)

This strenuous, rugged-and-wild hike on the coastal trail (SVA) will take you all the way into Levanto. Wear good shoes and bring lots of water.

Starting from Monterosso, look for signs for the coastal trail at the west end of the new town, and head steeply up. You'll hike up and over Punta Mesco, the bluff that separates the two towns. The first stretch, out of Monterosso, is almost entirely big steps; the rest is mostly a gradual up-and-down.

For a short scenic detour, look for trail #591 not far out of Monterosso. This brief jog leads to the ruined chapel of Sant'Antonio.

To begin the hike in Levanto, see page 123.

Alternate Routes: You can enjoy a **higher hike** by skipping the steepest stretch and riding one of Monterosso's shuttle buses to Colle di Gritta (and Hotel Monterosso Alto). From there, follow trail #591 along the ridge and down to Colle di Bagari, where several trails intersect. You can follow trail #571c from here or go a little lower to #571—both head down to trail SVA and Levanto. Or, to make your **hike a loop** that returns directly to Monterosso, continue from Colle di Bagari along trail #591 to trail SVA, and drop steeply into Monterosso.

▲Levanto-Bonassola (30 minutes)

For an easy excursion, take the train to Levanto, then stroll (or better yet, bike) the level, rails-to-trails promenade to the beach town of Bonassola (see page 124).

▲Bonassola-Framura (30 minutes)

From Bonassola (described above), the path (good for biking) continues through a series of tunnels to Framura, a cluster of small villages. You can take the scenic coastal trail to a small beach or hike up the road to the villages.

To the South
▲Riomaggiore-Porto Venere (6 hours, 8 miles)

For this challenging trek, you'll hike up from Riomaggiore on trail #593 (a continuation of the coastal trail SVA) to the sanctuary at Montenero, then up to Colle del Telegrafo; and then all the way down to Porto Venere on trail AV5T. Partway along, the town of Campiglia has a little bar/restaurant (and buses to La Spezia).

Long, Cross-Regional Hike
▲▲High Route Between Porto Venere and Levanto (22 miles)

Above the coastal trails, and higher than the sanctuary trails, is the

A level promenade links Levanto to Bonassola.

You can hike to sanctuaries and cemeteries above each of the five towns.

demanding 22-mile AV5T trail (*alta via 5 Terre,* also labeled trail #1 or #591/598). It connects Porto Venere to Levanto, offering sky-high views over the Cinque Terre seafront. Also called the Red Trail, it's cool, un-crowded, and at the top of the world. You could do all or part of this trail.

Other Cinque Terre Walks and Hikes

For each Cinque Terre town, I include a **self-guided walk** to help you explore the town (anytime, day or night). Manarola's is the most sce-nic, offering an easy, rewarding stroll through vineyards with stun-ning views. Per town, I also list a few easy hiking options, even as simple as walking just outside town to get a lovely overview.

Sanctuary Trails (La Strada dei Santuari)

Each of the five towns has its own sanctuary (with a chapel or church dedicated to the Virgin Mary), hovering in the hills a mile or two above town, and accessible by a long, steep hike (quiet and uncrowded). The sanctuaries were a place of refuge for each village in the age of pirate attacks.

Villagers feel deeply connected to these spiritual retreats, where they remember lost relatives and feel part of a timeless community. A network of "sanctuary trails" (no hiking card required) crisscrosses the hills above the main coastal route. There's no single path, but with a good map you can link up these moderately difficult trails. In most towns, the shuttle bus can take you from the town center to the sanc-tuary—you could ride up and hike down (described with each town's coverage, next).

Monterosso al Mare

This is a resort town with a few cars and lots of hotels, rentable beach umbrellas, crowds, and a little more late-night action than the neighboring towns. Monterosso al Mare—the only Cinque Terre town with some flat land—has two parts: A new town (called Fegina) with a parking lot, train station, and TI; and an old town (Centro Storico), which cradles Old World charm in its small, crooked lanes. In the old town, you'll find hole-in-the-wall shops, rustic pastel townscapes, and a new generation of creative small-businesspeople eager to keep their visitors happy. A handy pedestrian tunnel connects the old with the new.

ORIENTATION TO MONTEROSSO

Strolling Monterosso's waterfront promenade, you can pick out each of the Cinque Terre towns decorating the coast. After dark, they sparkle. Monterosso is the most enjoyable of the five for backpackers or the young-at-heart wanting to connect with others looking for a little nightlife.

Tourist Information

The TI, called Proloco Monterosso, is on the street below the train station (daily 9:00-18:30, longer hours in summer, shorter hours off-season, baggage storage, exit station and go left a few doors, tel. 0187-817-506, www.prolocomonterosso.it). A Cinque Terre park info desk and a ticket office are upstairs within the station near platform 1 (both usually daily 8:00-20:00, shorter hours off-season).

Arrival in Monterosso

By Train: Train travelers arrive in the new town. To reach most of my recommended hotels in the new town, turn right from the station. To get to the old town, turn left from the station, follow the seafront promenade, then duck through the tunnel just before the point—it's a scenic, flat 10-minute stroll.

The bar at track 1 (serving salads, sandwiches, and drinks) overlooks the tracks and the beach, and is a handy place with a cool breeze to hang out while waiting for a train. As many trains run late, this can turn a frustration into a blessing.

Taxis usually wait outside the train station, but if not, you can call one (€10 from station to old town, mobile 335-616-5842, 335-616-5845,

Walk Monterosso's beach promenade...

...or head uphill for an overview.

or 335-628-0933). ATC **shuttle buses** also go to the old town and are cheaper, but only run about once an hour.

By Car: Monterosso is 30 minutes off the freeway (exit: Carrodano-Levanto). About three miles above Monterosso, there's an intersection where you must choose either *Monterosso Centro Storico* (old part of town) or *Monterosso Fegina* (new town and beachfront parking). Know where you want to go, because you can't drive directly between the new town and old center (the tunnel is closed to most cars).

Get directions from your hotelier. Most drivers should choose the *Fegina* fork. Parking is easy (except July-Aug and weekends in June) in the new town in the huge beachfront guarded lot (€25/24 hours). In the old town, you'll find the Loreto parking garage on Via Roma, from which it's a 10-minute downhill walk to the main square (€2/hour, €20/24 hours).

Helpful Hints

Medical Help: The town's bike-riding, leather bag-toting, English-speaking physician is **Dr. Vitone** (simple visit-€50-100, less for poor students, mobile 338-853-0949, vitonee@yahoo.it).

Market: Every Thursday morning (8:00-13:00), trucks pull into the old town and fill the public area by the beach with stalls.

Baggage Storage: The **TI** will store bags (€6/day).

Laundry: For full-service, same-day laundry in the new town, try **Wash and Dry Lavarapido.** They'll pick up at your hotel, or you can drop it at their shop. The owners speak little English, so ask your hotelier to arrange the details (daily 9:00-19:00, Via Molinelli 17, mobile 339-484-0940, Lucia and Ivano). In the old town, head to **Luètu Lavanderia,** uphill on Via Roma and across from the post office (daily 8:00-20:00, maybe later in summer, tel. 328-286-1908).

Massage: Physiotherapist **Giorgio Moggia** gives good massages (€70/hour, mobile 339-314-6127, giomogg@tin.it).

MONTEROSSO WALKS

These self-guided walks will introduce you to Monterosso. The first one, focusing on the mostly level town center, takes about 30 minutes. For the second one, you'll summit the adjacent hill—allow an hour or so.

Monterosso Harbor and Town Walk

▶ *Hike out from the dock in the old town and stand atop the concrete breakwater. (If you're arriving by boat, you'll disembark here.)*

Breakwater

From this point you can survey Monterosso's old town (straight ahead) and new town (stretching to the left, with train station and parking lot). Notice the bluff that separates old and new, and imagine how much harder your commute would be if the narrow road tethering these two towns were somehow cut off. It happened in the spring of 2013, when the wall below the hill-topping Capuchin church gave way in a landslide. For a time, the only way to connect the two halves of town by car was to drive six miles around; on foot, you had to hike up and over this hill.

Looking to the right, you can see all *cinque* of the *terre* from one spot: Vernazza, Corniglia (above the shore), Manarola, and a few buildings of Riomaggiore beyond that.

These days, the harbor hosts more paddleboats than fishing boats. Erosion is a major problem. The partial breakwater—the row of giant rocks in the middle of the harbor—is designed to save the beach from washing away. While old-timers remember a vast beach, their grandchildren truck in sand each spring to give tourists something to bask on. (The Nazis liked the Cinque Terre, too—find two of their bomb-hardened bunkers embedded in the bluff.)

The fancy four-star Hotel Porto Roca (the pink building high on the hill, on the far right of the harbor) marks the trail to Vernazza. High above, you see an example of the costly roads built in the 1980s to connect the Cinque Terre towns with the freeway over the hills.

The two prominent capes (Punta di Montenero to the right, and Punta Mesco to the left) define the Cinque Terre region. The closer Punta Mesco is part of a protected marine sanctuary and home to a rare sea grass that provides an ideal home for fish eggs. Buoys keep

Arriving in Monterosso by boat

Church of St. John the Baptist

fishing boats away. The cape was once a quarry, providing employment to locals who chipped out the stones used to build the local towns (the greenish stones making up part of the breakwater are from there).

On the far end of the new town, marking the best free beach around, you can just see the statue named *Il Gigante* (hard to spot because it blends in with the gray rock). It's 45 feet tall and once held a trident. While it looks as if it were hewn from the rocky cliff, it's actually made of reinforced concrete and dates from the beginning of the 20th century, when it supported a dancing terrace for a *fin de siècle* villa. A violent storm left the giant holding nothing but memories of Monterosso's glamorous age.

▶ *From the breakwater, walk toward the old town and under the train tracks. Then venture right into the square and find the statue of a dandy holding what looks like a box cutter (near the big playground).*

Piazza Garibaldi

The statue honors Giuseppe Garibaldi, the dashing firebrand revolutionary who, in the 1860s, helped unite the people of Italy into a modern nation. Facing Garibaldi, with your back to the sea, you'll see (on your right) the orange City Hall (with the European Union flag beside the Italian one). You'll also see A Ca' du Sciensa restaurant, which has historic town photos inside and upstairs; you're welcome to pop in for a look.

Just under the bell tower (with your back to the sea, it's on your left), a set of covered arcades facing the sea is where the old-timers hang out (they see all and know all). The crenellated bell tower marks the church; it was originally the tower of a fortified gate.

▶ *Go to church.*

Accommodations

1. Hotel Villa Steno
2. Il Giardino Incantato
3. Hotel Pasquale
4. Locanda il Maestrale
5. Hotel la Colonnina
6. Albergo Marina
7. Buranco Agriturismo
8. Manuel's Guesthouse
9. L'Antica Terrazza & Gastronomia "San Martino"
10. Albergo al Carugio
11. La Villa degli Argentieri
12. To Hotel Villa Adriana
13. Hotel la Spiaggia & Bar Giò
14. A Cà du Gigante
15. Hotel Punta Mesco
16. Pensione Agavi
17. Affittacamere Rist. Il Gabbiano
18. Le Sirene/Raggi di Sole

Eateries & Nightlife

19. Ristorante Belvedere
20. Il Casello
21. L'Ancora della Tortuga & Torre Aurora
22. Via Venti
23. L'Osteria & Emy's Way Pizzeria Friggitoria
24. Ristorante al Pozzo
25. Ciak
26. Páe Veciu
27. La Smorfia & Pasticceria Laura
28. Miky
29. La Cantina di Miky
30. Il Frantoio Focacceria

Monterosso al Mare

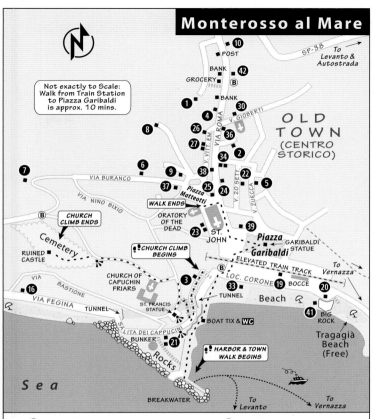

Not exactly to Scale:
Walk from Train Station
to Piazza Garibaldi
is approx. 10 mins.

To Levanto &
Autostrada

SP-38

10 POST

BANK
42
GROCERY
B
BANK

1

4
30
V. GIOBERTI

OLD
TOWN
(CENTRO
STORICO)

8

26
36
V. VITT. EM.
27

34
2

6
9
38
22
5
37
25
V. 20 SETT.
24
V. ZUECCA
Piazza
Matteotti

WALK ENDS

7

VIA BURANCO
VIA NINO BIXIO

ORATORY
OF THE
DEAD

23
ST.
JOHN
39

B

CHURCH CLIMB ENDS
Cemetery

RUINED
CASTLE

CHURCH CLIMB
BEGINS

Piazza
Garibaldi
GARIBALDI
STATUE

To
Vernazza

ELEVATED TRAIN TRACK

VIA
BASTIONE
16
VIA FEGINA
TUNNEL

CHURCH OF
CAPUCHIN FRIARS

ST. FRANCIS
STATUE

3

B
LOC. CORONE
33
TUNNEL
19 BOCCE
20

Beach

41
BIG
ROCK

SALITA DEI CAPPUCCINI

BUNKER
21
Rocks

BOAT TIX & WC

HARBOR & TOWN
WALK BEGINS

Tragagià
Beach
(Free)

Sea

BREAKWATER

To
Levanto

To
Vernazza

---

31 Il Massimo della Focaccia

32 La Bottega SMA

33 Bar Alga

34 Wonderland Bakery & Bar Davi

35 Bar il Baretto & Stella
Marina Beach Bar

36 Enoteca Internazionale
Wine Tasting

37 Enoteca da Eliseo

38 Fast Bar

39 El Dorado Wine Bar

40 Nuovo Eden Bar

41 Beach Bar Alga

42 Launderette (2)

Cinque Terre Flood and Recovery

On October 25, 2011, after a dry summer, a heavy rainstorm hit the Cinque Terre. Within four hours, 22 inches of rain fell. Flash floods rushed down the hillsides, picking up mud, rocks, trees, furniture, and even cars and buses in their raging, destructive path through the streets down to the sea. Part of Monterosso's old town and Vernazza's main drag were buried under a dozen feet of mud. Four villagers from Vernazza lost their lives.

Today, the Cinque Terre is back to normal. Most visitors wouldn't even notice that in the affected areas of Monterosso and Vernazza, everything is new: stoves, tables, chairs, and plates. Strolling through these towns today, appreciate the resilience of the human spirit (and the importance of good drainage).

Church of St. John the Baptist (Chiesa di San Giovanni Battista)

First, walk along the right side the church. Near the second side door, find the high-water mark (*altezza massima*) from an October 1966 flood—which also famously devastated Florence. Nearby, a second (higher) plaque commemorates the 2011 flood.

Now hook left, around the church—and appreciate its black-and-white-striped main facade. With white marble from Carrara and green marble from Punta Mesco, the church is typical of the region's Gothic style. The church's marble stripes get narrower the higher they go, creating the illusion that the church is taller than it really is. Note the lacy, stone rose window above the entrance—considered one of the finest in northern Italy. It's as delicate as crochet work, with 18 slender columns (creating the petals of the rose).

Step inside for more Ligurian Gothic: original marble columns and capitals with pointed arches to match. The octagonal baptismal font (in the back of the church) was carved from Carrara marble in

1359. Imagine the job getting that from the quarries, about 40 miles away. The fine Baroque altar was crafted with various marbles from around Italy in the 1700s. The church itself dates from 1307—the proud inscription on the left-middle column reads "MilloCCCVII."

▶ *Leaving the church, turn left and go to church again.*

Oratory of the Dead (Oratorio dei Neri)

During the Counter-Reformation, the Catholic Church offset the rising influence of the Lutherans by creating brotherhoods of good works. These religious Rotary clubs were called "confraternities." Monterosso had two, nicknamed White and Black. This building is the oratory of the Black group, whose mission—as the macabre decor filling the interior indicates—was to arrange for funerals and take care of widows, orphans, the shipwrecked, and the souls of those who ignore the request for a €1 donation. It dates from the 16th century, and membership has passed from father to son for generations. Notice the fine, carved pews (c. 1700), just inside the door, and the haunted-house chandeliers. Look up at the ceiling to find the symbol of the confraternity: a skull-and-crossbones and an hourglass...death awaits us all.

▶ *On that cheery note, if you're in a lazy mood, you can end your walking tour here to enjoy strolling, shopping, gelato-licking, a day at the beach...or all of the above. But if you're up for a hike, face out to sea, look to the right and imagine the view from the top of that hill. Now... go see it.*

Capuchin Church and Climb

The hill that separates the old town from the new rewards anyone who climbs up with a peaceful church, a cemetery in the clouds, and a panoramic view.

▶ *From the old town's beachfront, find the brick steps squeezed between Hotel Pasquale and its restaurant, and start climbing. The lane is signed Salita dei Cappuccini (nicknamed Zii di Frati), or...*

Switchbacks of the Friars

Follow the yellow brick road (OK, it's orange...but I couldn't help singing as I skipped skyward). Partway up, detour left to the terrace above the seaside castle at a statue of St. Francis and a wolf taking in a grand

St. Francis graces a Ligurian Sea viewpoint.

view. Enjoy an opportunity to see all five of the Cinque Terre towns. Then backtrack 20 yards to the switchback and continue uphill.

▶ *When you reach a gate marked Convento e Chiesa Cappuccini, you have arrived at the...*

Church of the Capuchin Friars

The former monastery is now manned by a single caretaker friar. (If you meet Father Renato, take a moment to speak with him—he's a joyful soul who loves to connect.) Before stepping inside, notice the church's striped Romanesque facade. It's all fake. Tap it—no marble, just cheap 18th-century stucco. Go inside and sit in the rear pew. The high altarpiece painting of St. Francis can be rolled up on special days to reveal a statue of Mary standing behind it.

The fine painting of the **Crucifixion** (on the left) recalls how, when Jesus died, the earth went dark. Notice the eclipsed sun in the painting, just to the right of the cross. Do the electric candles work? Pick one up, pray for peace, and plug it in. (Leave an offering, or unplug it and put it back.)

▶ *Leave and turn left through another gate to hike 100 yards uphill to*

the cemetery filling the ruined castle at the top of the hill. Reaching the
cemetery's gate, look back and enjoy the view over the town.

Cemetery in the Ruined Castle

In the Dark Ages, the village huddled behind this castle. As the threat of pirates passed, it slowly expanded to the waterfront. Notice the town view from here—no sea. You're looking at the oldest part of Monterosso, tucked behind the hill, out of view of 13th-century pirates.

Respectfully explore the cemetery. Ponder the black-and-white photos of grandparents past. Read the headstones: *Q.R.P.* is *Qui Riposa in Pace* (a.k.a. R.I.P.). Rich families had their own little tomb buildings. That this is still a place treasured by the living is demonstrated by the abundance of fresh flowers.

Climb to the very summit—the castle's keep, or place of last refuge. Priests are buried in a line of graves closest to the sea, but facing inland, looking toward the town's holy sanctuary high on the hillside (above the road, with its triangular steeple just peeking above the trees). Each Cinque Terre town has a lofty sanctuary, dedicated to Mary and dear to the village hearts.

▶ *Your tour is over—any trail leads you back into town.*

EXPERIENCES IN MONTEROSSO

Hikes from Monterosso

For a relatively easy in-town hike, take a rewarding climb up to the **hilltop cemetery** between the old and the new towns (described earlier).

Several ambitious hikes begin in Monterosso; you can use ATC **shuttle buses** to make challenging hikes easier (for details, see page 19).

If you're hiking to **Vernazza** on the main coastal trail, you'll need a park card (sold at the trailhead). If heading north over the Punta Mesco bluff to **Levanto,** you can take the bus up to Colle di Gritta—which makes most of the rest of the hike downhill. (For more on these hikes, see "Hiking the Cinque Terre," earlier.)

You can hike to Monterosso's **Soviore sanctuary** (on trail #509)

Monterosso's sandy new town beach is busy.   The gravel old town beach is less crowded.

or take the shuttle bus. To hike from Soviore to Vernazza's **Madonna di Reggio sanctuary,** follow a mostly level trail (#591) to Termine, then head down to Madonna di Reggio (on #582), then steeply downhill into Vernazza (on #508). Allow 2.5 hours, if you start with the shuttle bus.

Beaches

Monterosso's **new town** has easily the Cinque Terre's best—and most crowded—beach (immediately in front of the train station). Most of the beach is technically private, where (at Stella Marina) you'll pay €20 to rent two chairs and an umbrella for the day (prices get soft in the afternoon). Light lunches are served by beach cafés to sunbathers at their lounge chairs. Various outfits along here rent kayaks and stand-up paddleboards (look for signs at the west end of the beach—near the parking lot—or ask around). If there are no umbrellas on a stretch of beach, it's public (free), so you can spread out a towel anywhere. There's a free beach at the far west end, near the Gigante statue; others are marked on the "Monterosso al Mare" map, earlier.

The **old town** also has its own predominantly private beach; you can rent umbrellas, chairs, kayaks, and paddleboats from Beach Bar Alga, which is also a scenic spot for a drink. Tucked just beyond the private beach—under the Il Casello restaurant at the east end of town—is the free public beach called Tragagià, which is gravelly and generally less crowded (showers). The bocce ball court (next to Il Casello) is busy with older men enjoying their favorite pastime.

Wine Tasting

Buranco Agriturismo is one of the largest producers of wines in the Cinque Terre, with tastings on their terrace with views over the vineyards. You'll also taste grappa (firewater) and *limoncino*. It's best to call or email ahead to let them know you are coming (€20-30/person with snacks, tastings usually daily 12:00-18:00, follow Via Buranco uphill to path, 10 minutes above town, also rents recommended apartments, mobile 349-434-8046, www.burancocinqueterre.it, info@buranco.it, Mary).

Enoteca Internazionale is a good place in town to sample local wines. Mario serves a selection of five wines for €20 (his bruschetta makes a fine light meal as you're sipping, open daily until late, Via Roma 62, tel. 0187-817-278).

Boat Rides

In addition to the regularly scheduled big boats (see page 16), you can hire your own captain for transfers to other towns or for a lazy sightseeing cruise (if the water's calm).

Stefano has two six-person boats: the *Matilde* and the *Babaah* (about €100/hour, 90 minutes is enough for a quick spin, two hours includes time for swimming; longer trips to Porto Venere and offshore islands possible; mobile 333-821-2007, www.matildenavigazione.com, info@matildenavigazione.com).

Diego offers half-day, daylong, and sunset excursions for up to seven on his cushy boat. Longer tours can include snorkeling, village visits, and a buffet lunch (group tours—€70, daily 10:30-13:30 & 17:30-20:30, best to email or call to confirm and reserve; private tours—€120/hour for up to 4 people, €150/hour for 5-7 people; mobile 339-233-9297, www.cinqueterreboat.com, 5terretourfishandchill@gmail.com).

Sea Breeze Boat Tours arranges day and *aperitivo* sunset tours, and will shuttle you to any of the coastal towns. They also run tours from Levanto (€85-140/person, mobile 328-824-6889 or 338-809-9278, www.seabreezeboattours.com, info@seabreezeboattours.com, Matteo and Federica).

MONTEROSSO AL MARE

NIGHTLIFE IN MONTEROSSO

Although I've listed these establishments for their nightlife, they work any time of day for a drink and spot to relax.

Enoteca da Eliseo, my favorite wine bar in town, comes with operatic ambience. Eliseo and his wife, Mary, love music and wine. Taste by the glass *(bicchiere),* or select a fine bottle from their shop shelf, then enjoy the village action from their cozy tables. Eliseo stocks more than a hundred varieties of grappa (Wed-Mon 14:00-23:30, closed Tue, Piazza Matteotti 3, a block inland behind church, tel. 0187-817-308).

Fast Bar is super basic, but it's the best bar in town for young travelers and night owls. Customers mix travel tales with big, cold beers, and the crowd (and the rock 'n' roll) gets noisier as the night rolls on. Come here to watch Italian or American sporting events on TV all day (cheap *panini,* salads, and other light meals usually served until midnight, open 9:30-late, in the old town at Via Roma 13; Alex, Francesco, and Stefano).

La Cantina di Miky, in the new town just beyond the train station, is a trendy bar-restaurant with an extensive cocktail and grappa menu. The seating is in three zones: overlooking the beach, in the

Monterosso's beachfront is beautiful on a balmy evening.

garden, or in the cellar. Try the fun "five villages" wine tasting. This is the best place in town for top-end Italian microbrews (Thu-Tue until late, closed Wed, Via Fegina 90, tel. 0187-802-525).

El Dorado Wine Bar is the local old-town nighttime hangout. Set on a small piazza, it offers music, drinks and people-watching late into the night (Piazza Garibaldi 22, daily 10:00-2:00 in the morning, tel. 331-475-9611).

Beach Bars: On a balmy evening, enjoy a memorable drink with a view of swimmers, sunbathers, and the languid Ligurian Sea. In the new town, try **Nuovo Eden Bar,** overlooking the beach by the big rock (drinks come with a light snack, good ice cream). In the old town, **Beach Bar Alga** has an island ambience (all outside, daily until 20:00, Stefano).

SLEEPING IN MONTEROSSO

Monterosso, the most beach-resorty of the five Cinque Terre towns, offers maximum comfort and ease. Rooms in Monterosso are a better value than similar rooms in crowded Vernazza, and the proprietors seem more genuine and welcoming.

In the Old Town
$$$$ Hotel Villa Steno is lovingly managed and features panoramic gardens, a roof terrace with sun beds, and the friendly help of Matteo and his wife, Carla. Of the 16 rooms, 14 have great view balconies (RS%, air-con, family rooms, hearty breakfast, elevator, laundry service, ask about pay parking when you reserve, hike up to their panoramic terrace, closed Nov-March, Via Roma 109, tel. 0187-817-028 or 0187-818-336, www.villasteno.com, steno@pasini.com). It's a 15-minute climb (or €10 taxi ride) from the train station to the hotel. My readers get a free Cinque Terre info packet and a glass of local wine when they check in—ask.

$$$$ Il Giardino Incantato ("The Enchanted Garden") is a charming, comfortable four-room B&B in a tastefully renovated 16th-century Ligurian home in the heart of the old town. It's run by eager-to-please Fausto and Mariapia and their gregarious staff. Sip their homemade *limoncino* at *aperitivo* time, and have breakfast under lemon trees in the delightful hidden garden that's candlelit in the evening (air-con, free minibar and tea-and-coffee service, laundry, Via Mazzini 18, tel. 0187-818-315, mobile 333-264-9252, www.ilgiardino incantato.net, giardino_incantato@libero.it).

$$$$ Hotel Pasquale is modern and comfortable with 15 seaview rooms, run by the same family as Hotel Villa Steno (earlier). Located right on the harbor, it's just a few steps from the beach, boat dock, and tunnel to the new town. While there is some train noise, the soundtrack is mostly a lullaby of waves. It has an elevator and offers easier access than most (RS%, family room, air-con, laundry service, closed Nov-March, Via Fegina 4, tel. 0187-817-550 or 0187-817-477, www.hotelpasquale.it, pasquale@pasini.com, welcoming Felicita and Marco). Felicita also rents several well-equipped apartments in the center of the old town.

$$$ Locanda il Maestrale rents six stylish rooms in a sophisti-cated and peaceful little inn. Although renovated with all the modern comforts and thoughtful details, it retains centuries-old character under frescoed ceilings. Its peaceful sun terrace overlooking the old town and Via Roma action is a delight. Guests enjoy complimentary drinks and snacks each afternoon (air-con, Via Roma 37, tel. 0187-817-013, mobile 338-4530-531, www.locandamaestrale.net, maestrale@ monterossonet.com, Stefania and Giovanni).

$$$ Hotel la Colonnina has 22 big rooms with varying decor, generous and meticulously cared-for public spaces, a cozy garden, and an inviting shared seaview terrace with sun beds. It's buried in the town's fragrant and sleepy back streets (family rooms, all but one room has a private terrace, cash preferred but cards accepted, air-con, fridges, elevator, a block inland from main square at Via Zuecca 6, tel. 0187-817-439, www.lacolonninacinqueterre.it, info@lacolonnina cinqueterre.it, Cristina).

$$$ Albergo Marina, run by enthusiastic husband-and-wife team Marina and Eraldo, has 23 pleasant rooms and a garden with lemon trees. They serve a filling breakfast buffet and host a happy hour most days on their terrace. With lots of little extras, they offer a fine value (RS%, family rooms, elevator, air-con, fridges, free kayak and snorkel equipment, Via Buranco 40, tel. 0187-817-613, www.hotel marina5terre.com, marina@hotelmarina5terre.com).

$$$ Buranco Agriturismo, a 10-minute hike above the old town, has wonderful gardens and views over the vine-covered valley.

Its primary business is wine and olive-oil production (and they host wine tastings), but they also offer three apartments. It's a rare opportunity to stay in a farmhouse yet be able to walk to town (air-con, tel. 0187-817-677, mobile 349-434-8046, www.burancocinqueterre.it, info@buranco.it, informally run by Loredana, Mary, and Giulietta).

$$$ Manuel's Guesthouse, perched high above the town among terraces, is a garden getaway run by Lorenzo and his father, Giovanni. They have six big, artfully decorated rooms and a grand view. After climbing the killer stairs from the town center, their killer terrace is hard to leave—especially after a few drinks (cash only, air-con, up about 100 steps behind church—you can ask Lorenzo to carry your bags up, Via San Martino 39, mobile 333-439-0809, www.manuels guesthouse.com, manuelsguesthouse@libero.it).

$$ L'Antica Terrazza rents four tight, classy rooms right in town. With a pretty terrace overlooking the pedestrian street, Raffaella and John offer a good deal (single room with private bath down the hall, air-con, Vicolo San Martino 1, mobile 347-132-6213, www.antica terrazza.com, post@anticaterrazza.com).

$ Albergo al Carugio has nine practical rooms in a big apartment-style building at the top of the old town. It's quiet, comfy, and a fine budget value; one room has a private terrace (no breakfast, air-con, fridges, Via Roma 100, tel. 0187-817-453, www.alcarugio.it, info@ alcarugio.it, conscientiously run by Andrea).

In the New Town

$$$$ La Villa degli Argentieri offers 11 spacious rooms, many with balconies, from the quiet end of the beachfront street. From the front rooms you'll get a peek-a-boo look (through trees) at the water, but the inviting rooftop terrace with sunbeds has panoramic views (air-con, elevator, Via Fegina 120, tel. 0187-818-963, www.lavilladegli argentieri.it, info@lavilladegliargentieri.it).

$$$$ Hotel Villa Adriana is big, contemporary, and bright, set on a church-owned estate with a peaceful garden, a pool, free parking, and a no-stress style. They rent 55 sterile rooms—some with terraces and/or sea views—ask when you reserve, but no guarantees (family rooms, air-con, elevator, loaner bikes, room fridges, affordable dinners, Via IV Novembre 23, tel. 0187-818-109, www.villaadriana.info, info@villaadriana.info).

$$$$ Hotel la Spiaggia, facing the beach, is a venerable place with 19 rooms (half with sea views) and a quiet garden retreat (cash only, air-con, elevator, free parking—reserve in advance, Via Lungomare 96, tel. 0187-817-567, www.laspiaggiahotel5terre.com, laspiaggiahotel@gmail.com, Maria). They also rent four pricey, ultra-mod rooms on the seafront promenade.

$$$$ A Cà du Gigante, despite its name, is a tiny yet chic refuge with nine rooms, all on the ground floor. About 100 yards from the beach (and surrounded by blocky apartments), the interior is tastefully done with upscale comfort in mind (air-con, limited pay parking—reserve ahead, Via IV Novembre 11, tel. 0187-817-401, www.ilgigante cinqueterre.it, gigante@ilgigantecinqueterre.it, Claudia).

$$$ Hotel Punta Mesco is a tidy, well-run little haven renting 17 quiet, casual rooms at a good price. While none have views, 10 rooms have small terraces (family room, air-con, parking, Via Molinelli 35, tel. 0187-817-495, www.hotelpuntamesco.it, info@hotelpuntamesco. it, Roberto, Diego, and Manuel).

$$ Pensione Agavi has eight spartan, bright, overpriced rooms along the waterfront promenade. I'd skip it—unless you can score one of the rooms with a grand view over the beach (RS%, cheaper rooms with shared bath, expensive breakfast, refrigerators, no kids, turn left out of station to Via Fegina 30, tel. 0187-817-171, www.hotelagavi.com, info@hotelagavi.com, Hillary).

$$ Affittacamere Ristorante il Gabbiano, a touristy restaurant on the beachfront road, rents five basic, dated, but affordable rooms up-stairs. Three face the sea (two with small balconies); two have terraces overlooking a garden. Check in at the restaurant (big family rooms, cash only, no breakfast, air-con, Via Fegina 84, tel. 0187-817-578, www.affitta camereristorante-ilgabbiano.com, lella-v71@hotmail.it, Raffaella).

$ Le Sirene/Raggi di Sole, with nine simple rooms in two humble buildings, is a decent budget choice. It's run from a hole-in-the-wall re-ception desk a block from the station, just off the water. I'd request the more spacious Le Sirene building, with smaller bathrooms but no train noise (RS%, family rooms, fans, Via Molinelli 1A, mobile 331-788-1088 or 329-595-1063, www.sirenerooms.com, sirenerooms@gmail.com, Ermanna).

EATING IN MONTEROSSO

With a Sea View

$$ Ristorante Belvedere, big and sprawling, serves good-value meals indoors or outdoors on the harborfront. Their huge €49 *anfora belvedere*—mixed seafood stew dumped dramatically at the table from a pottery amphora into your bowl—can easily be split among four diners. Their *misto mare* plate (2-person minimum, €16/person), a fishy treat, nearly makes an entire meal. It's energetically run by Federico and Roberto (Wed-Mon 12:00-14:30 & 18:00-22:00, closed Tue, on the harbor in the old town, tel. 0187-817-033).

$$ Il Casello offers outdoor terrace seating only, on a little bluff overlooking the old town beach when the weather's nice. It's a pleasant spot for pasta, seafood, or a drink (daily 12:00-22:00, mobile 333-492-7629, Bacco).

$$$ L'Ancora della Tortuga is a top option in Monterosso for seaview elegance, with gorgeous outdoor seating high on a bluff and a white-tablecloth-and-candles interior fit for an admiral. While the food and service can be three-star, the setting is five-star. Drop by to choose and reserve a table for later (Tue-Sun 12:30-15:30 & 18:30-21:30, closed Mon and when stormy; at the tip of the point between the old and new towns—just outside the tunnel; tel. 0187-800-065, mobile 333-240-7956, Silvia and Giamba).

$$$$ Torre Aurora is a top-end, fancy restaurant with no indoor seating. You'll dine outside (wrapped in a blanket if it's cold) around the medieval tower with commanding views of the sea while enjoying simple yet creative dishes. Reservations are smart (daily in good weather, mobile 366-145-3702, www.torreauroracinqueterre.com, Elia). They serve cocktails outside of mealtime.

In the Old Town

$$$ Via Venti is a quiet little trattoria, hidden in an alley deep in the heart of the old town, where chef Ilaria and her husband Michele create and serve imaginative seafood dishes. Be tempted by their delicate and savory gnocchi with crab, tender ravioli stuffed with fresh fish, and pear-and-pecorino pasta. The outdoor tables are on a lane as nondescript as the humdrum interior—but you're here for the food (Fri-Wed 12:00-14:30 & 18:30-22:30, closed Thu, Via XX Settembre 32, tel. 0187-818-347).

$ Gastronomia "San Martino," warmly run by hardworking Moreno and Sabrina, is a tiny, humble combination of takeaway and sit-down café with surprisingly affordable, quality dishes. Belly up to the glass case and see what's cooking, then eat at one of the few tables—inside or out on a pleasant street. You're welcome to create your own €13 mixed plate by pointing to whatever appeals (Tue-Sun 12:00-15:00 & 18:00-22:00, closed Mon, next to recommended L'Antica Terrazza hotel at Vicolo San Martino 3, mobile 346-109-7338).

$$ L'Osteria is a delightful little family-run place serving "cuisine with passion" at wonderful prices. Their Possa wine, from vineyards close to the sea, is the oyster of local wines, or maybe it's just the Ligurian music (Tue-Sun lunch served 12:00-14:30, evening seatings at 19:00 and 21:00, closed Mon, Via Vittorio Emanuele 5, tel. 0187-819-224). It's a cozy scene inside with a few tables outside in the shadow of the church.

$$$ Ristorante al Pozzo is a favorite among locals. It's family-run, with good old-fashioned quality, as Gino (with his long white beard) cooks, and his English-speaking son, Manuel, serves. They have one of the best wine lists in town, serve only homemade pasta, and are known for their raw fish and wonderful seafood *antipasti misti* (Fri-Wed 12:00-15:00 & 18:30-22:30, closed Thu, Via Roma 24, tel. 0187-817-575).

$$$ Ciak, high-energy and tightly packed—inside and out—is a local institution with reliably good food, higher prices, and (sometimes) a bit of an attitude. Stroll a couple of paces past the outdoor tables up Via Roma to see what Signore Ciak (who wears his Popeye cap in the kitchen) has on the stove (Thu-Tue 12:00-15:00 & 18:00-22:30, closed Wed, Piazza Don Minzoni 6, tel. 0187-817-014).

$$ Páe Veciu, tucked away from the hubbub, has a short, creative menu of well-prepared seafood, pastas, a few meat dishes, and a good selection of local wines. Eat inside in view of the kitchen or at one of the few streetside tables (daily 11:30-15:00 & 18:30-22:00, Via Vittorio Emanuele 69, mobile 327-941-0430).

$ La Smorfia—a local favorite—cooks up good pizza in a sloppy setting that somehow says, "Great pizza enjoyed here." Their large pizzas can feed three (Fri-Wed 11:00-24:00, closed Thu, Via Vittorio Emanuele 73, tel. 0187-818-395).

In the New Town

$$$$ Miky is packed with a well-dressed clientele who know their seafood. For elegantly presented, top-quality food that celebrates local ingredients and traditions, it's worth the steep prices. It's a proud family operation—Miky (dad), Simonetta (mom), charming Sara (daughter, who greets guests)—and the attentive waitstaff all work hard. Many of their fine wines are available by the glass. Their mixed dessert sampler plate, *dolce misto,* serves two and is a fitting capper (Wed-Mon 12:00-15:00 & 19:00-23:00, closed Tue, reservations wise, in the new town 100 yards from train station at Via Fegina 104, tel. 0187-817-608, www.ristorantemiky.it).

$$$ La Cantina di Miky, a few doors down from the station, serves artfully crafted Ligurian specialties that follow in Miky's family tradition of quality. Run by son Manuel—and Christine from New Jersey—it's youthful and informal (sit downstairs, in the garden, or on the promenade overlooking the sea). The €20 anchovy tasting plate is an education (creative desserts, large selection of Italian microbrews, Thu-Tue 12:00-24:00, closed Wed, Via Fegina 90, tel. 0187-802-525). This place doubles as a cocktail bar in the evenings.

Light Meals, Takeout Food, and Breakfast

In the Old Town: Lots of shops and bakeries sell pizza and focaccia to eat in or take out for an easy picnic on the beach or trail. At **$ Il Frantoio Focacceria,** Simone makes tasty pizza and focaccia (Fri-Wed 9:00-14:00 & 16:30-20:00, closed Thu, just off Via Roma at Via Gioberti 1). **$ Emy's Way Pizzeria Friggitoria** offers pasta, thick-crust pizza (whole and by the slice), and deep-fried seafood in to-go cones (daily 11:00-20:00, later in summer, along the skinny street next to the church, tel. 331-788-1088, Emiliano).

In the New Town, near the Station: For a quick bite right at the train station (or on the beach), try **$ Il Massimo della Focaccia** for quiche-like tortes, sandwiches, focaccia pizzas, and desserts. With benches just in front, this is a good bet for a light meal with a sea view (Thu-Tue 9:00-19:00, closed Wed except June-Aug, Via Fegina 50 at the station). **La Bottega SMA** is a smart minimart with fresh produce, *antipasti,* deli items, and other picnic fare (daily 8:00-13:00 & 16:30-19:30 except closed Sun afternoon, shorter hours off-season, near Lavarapido at Vittoria Gianni 21).

Breakfast: Most hotels include breakfast in the room rate, but a handful leave you to your own devices. In the **old town,** for breakfast on the beach, try **Bar Alga** (from 8:00 when the weather's nice). For the freshest bakery items, follow your nose to **Pasticceria Laura,** serving coffee and pastries daily from 7:00 (Via Vittorio Emanuele 59), or head to the **Wonderland Bakery,** offering croissants, biscotti, and savory bites to go (from 8:00, Via San Pietro 8). **Bar Davi** has the biggest menu, serving bacon and eggs, yogurt, fruit, and cereal from 8:00 (pastries and coffee available from 7:00, under the arch at Via Roma 34).

In the **new town,** these places (on Via Fegina, near Hotel la Spiaggia) serve something akin to breakfast starting at 8:00: **Bar Giò** (bacon and eggs), **Bar il Baretto** (bacon and eggs), and **Stella Marina Beach Bar** (croissants and yogurt—served down on the beach). Your best bet might be a picnic breakfast from the tiny *alimentari*/supermarket at Via Fegina 116 (cheeses, breads, pastries, and fruit).

MONTEROSSO CONNECTIONS

Of the five Cinque Terre towns, Monterosso has the most direct train connections with towns outside the Cinque Terre.

From Monterosso by Train to: Levanto (3-4/hour, 4 minutes), **Sestri Levante** (hourly, 30 minutes, most trains to Genoa stop here), **Santa Margherita Ligure** (at least hourly, 45 minutes), **Genoa** (hourly, 1.5 hours; for destinations in France, you'll change trains here), **Milan** (8/day direct, otherwise hourly with change in Genoa, 3 hours), **Venice** (5/day, 6 hours, change in Milan), **La Spezia** (2-3/hour, 15-30 minutes), **Pisa** (hourly, 1-1.5 hours), **Rome** (hourly, 4.5 hours, change in La Spezia).

Vernazza

With the closest thing to a natural harbor—overseen by a ruined castle, a stout stone church, and a pastel canyon of fisherfolk homes—Vernazza is the jewel of the Cinque Terre. Only the regular noisy slurping up of the train by the mountain reminds you of the modern world. The action is at the harbor, where you'll find outdoor eateries ringing a humble piazza, a restaurant hanging on the edge of the castle, and a breakwater with a promenade, corralled by a natural amphitheater of terraced hills.

Join (or sit on a bench and watch) the locals devoting their leisure time to taking part in the *passeggiata*—strolling lazily together up and down the main street, doing *vasche* (laps). Learn—and live—the phrase *"la vita pigra di Vernazza"* (the lazy life of Vernazza).

Proud of their Vernazzan heritage, the town's residents like to brag: "Vernazza is locally owned. Portofino has sold out." Fearing change, keep-Vernazza-small proponents stopped the construction of a major road into the town and region. Families are tight and go back centuries; you'll notice certain surnames (such as Basso and Moggia) everywhere. In the winter, the population shrinks, as many people return to more-comfortable big-city apartments to spend the money they earned during the tourist season.

During the day in season the tiny harborfront and one main street are clogged with gawking group excursions. But early and late Vernazza is the cool and content domain of locals...and travelers who are lucky enough to call the town home for a couple of nights.

Tourist Information

At the train station, you can get answers to basic questions at the gift shop/park office (daily 8:00-20:00, closed in winter, tel. 0187-812-533, WCs just down the track, see "Helpful Hints," below, for baggage storage).

Arrival in Vernazza

By Train: Vernazza's train station is only about three train cars long, but the trains themselves are much longer, so most cars come to a stop in a long, dimly lit tunnel. Get out anyway, and walk through the tunnel—heading for the light—to reach the station. From there the main street flows through town right down to the harbor. If you're sleeping here, many locals who rent rooms will meet you at the station and walk you to your place (call ahead to tell them which train you're on).

By Car: Don't drive to Vernazza. Roads to Vernazza are in terrible shape, and parking is strictly limited. If you're coming from the north, park in Levanto. If arriving from the south, park in La Spezia. From either town, hop on the train.

Helpful Hints

Market: Vernazza's skimpy business community is augmented Tuesday mornings (8:00-13:00), when a meager gang of cars and trucks pulls into town for a tailgate market. Eros is often among the vendors; his family has sold flowers here for years (and he's also an amazing opera singer).

Baggage Storage: You can pay to leave your bags at the train station TI/gift shop (daily 9:00-19:00, closed in winter). The staff will also happily haul your luggage between the train station and your accommodations (€4/piece).

Laundry: A small self-serve launderette is at the top of town next to the post office (daily 9:00-22:00).

Booking Agency: Cinque Terre Riviera, run by Miriana, books vacation rentals in the Cinque Terre towns and La Spezia. They also sell tickets for Vernazza's summer opera and can arrange transportation, cooking classes, and weddings (Via Roma 24, tel. 0187-812-123, mobile 340-794-7358, www.cinqueterreriviera.com).

Massage: Kate Allen offers a relaxing fusion of aromatic/Swedish/holistic massage and reflexology in her studio in the center across from the pharmacy (tel. 0187-812-537, mobile 333-568-4653, www.vernazzamassage5terre.com).

Vernazza's pastel palette is chosen by a commissioner of good taste.

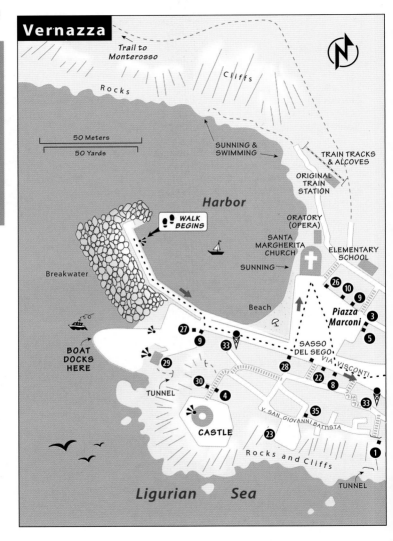

Vernazza

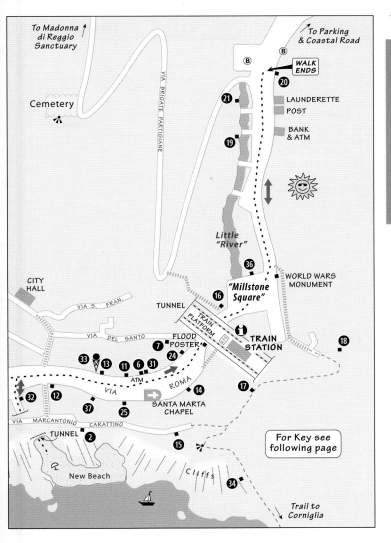

To Madonna di Reggio Sanctuary

To Parking & Coastal Road

WALK ENDS

B   B

20

Cemetery

21

LAUNDERETTE

POST

19

BANK & ATM

VIA BRIGATE PARTIGIANE

Little "River"

36

CITY HALL

16   World Wars Monument

"Millstone Square"

VIA S. FRAN.

TUNNEL

TRAIN PLATFORM

VIA DEL SANTO

FLOOD POSTER

TRAIN STATION

7

18

33   13

11 6 31

24

ATM

ROMA

17

32   12

VIA

14

37   25

SANTA MARTA CHAPEL

VIA MARCANTONIO CARATTINO

TUNNEL

2

15

For Key see following page

New Beach

Cliffs

34

Trail to Corniglia

Vernazza Map Key

See map on previous page.

Accommodations

1 La Malà & La Marina Rooms
2 Vernazza sul Mare
3 Nicolina Rooms Reception & Ristorante Pizzeria Vulnetia
4 Monica Lercari Rooms
5 Francamaria Reception & Albergo Barbara Rooms
6 Emanuela Colombo Rooms
7 Vernazza Rooms Reception
8 Rosa Vitali Rooms
9 Maria Capellini Rooms (2)
10 Martina Callo Rooms, Capitano Rooms Reception & Trattoria del Capitano
11 Rooms Francesca Reception (Enoteca Sciacchetrà)
12 Ivo's Camere
13 Memo Rooms
14 Eva's Rooms & Trattoria da Sandro
15 Rooms Elisabetta
16 Manuela Moggia Rooms
17 Casa Cato
18 Giuliano Basso Rooms
19 Camere Fontanavecchia
20 Tonino Basso/La Perla Rooms & Il Pirata delle Cinque Terre Café
21 La Rosa dei Venti
22 Gianni Franzi Reception/Ristorante
23 Gianni Franzi Rooms

Eateries & Other

24 Blue Marlin Bar
25 Lunch Box
26 Ananasso Bar
27 Pizzeria Baia Saracena
28 Gambero Rosso
29 Ristorante Belforte
30 Ristorante al Castello
31 Antica Osteria il Baretto
32 Pizzeria Ercole
33 Gelateria (3)
34 Bar la Torre
35 Vernazza Wine Experience
36 Cinque Sensi Wine Tastings
37 Cinque Terre Riviera Agency (Room Rental; Opera Tickets)

VERNAZZA WALK

This self-guided walk gives you a quick overview of the town. To trace the route, see the map on the previous page.

▶ *From the train station, walk downhill and all the way out onto the breakwater. Find a comfortable and safe place to sit and get to know Vernazza.*

The Town

Before the 11th century, pirates made this coast uninhabitable, so the first Vernazzans lived in the hills above. The earliest references call the town "Fortress Vernazza." Its towers, fortified walls, and hillside terracing date mostly from the 12th through 15th century. That's when the threat of pirates subsided and people felt comfortable coming out of the hills. Vernazza allied itself with the Republic of Genoa, a maritime power of the day. The **big red central building** facing the harbor was once the site where Genoan warships were built (12th century; to help identify it, see the photo on page 61).

In the Middle Ages, there was no beach or square. The water went right up to the buildings, where boats would tie up, Venetian-style. Imagine what Vernazza looked like in those days, when it was the biggest and richest of the Cinque Terre towns. Buildings had a water gate (facing today's square) and a front door on the higher inland side. There was no pastel plaster—just fine stonework (traces of which survive above Trattoria del Capitano). The town, hiding behind its little bluff, was camouflaged by its gray stonework—certainly not gaily painted to attract the eyes of marauding pirates. But apart from the added paint and plaster, the general shape and size of the town has changed little in five centuries.

Vernazza has two halves. *Sciuiu* (Vernazzan dialect for "flowery") is the sunny side on the left, and *luvegu* (dank) is the shady side on the right. Houses below the castle were connected by an interior arcade—ideal for fleeing attacks.

The "Ligurian pastel" colors of the buildings are regulated by the regional government's commissioner of good taste. The square before you is known for some of the area's finest restaurants.

While the town has 1,500 residents in summer, only 500 stay here through the winter. Vernazza has accommodations for about that many tourists.

Above Town

The small, **round tower** above the red building is another part of the city fortifications, reminding us of the town's importance in the Middle Ages. Back then, Genoa's enemies (rival maritime republics, especially Pisa) were Vernazza's enemies. That tower recalls a time when the town was fortified by a stone wall.

Vineyards fill the mountainside beyond the town. Notice the many terraces. For six centuries, the economy was based on wine and olive oil. Then came the 1980s—and the tourists. Locals turned to tourism to make a living, and stopped tending the land and vineyards.

Although many locals still maintain their small plots and proudly serve their family wines, the patchwork of vineyards is atomized and complex because of inheritance traditions. Historically, families divided their land among their children. Parents wanted each child to receive good land, though some lots were "kissed by the sun" while others were shady. Lots were split into increasingly tiny, unviable pieces, and many were eventually abandoned. The vineyards once stretched as high as you can see, but since fewer people sweat in the fields these days, the most distant terraces have gone wild again.

Church, School, and City Hall

Vernazza's Ligurian Gothic **church,** built with black stones quarried from Punta Mesco (the distant point between Monterosso and Levanto), dates from 1318. Note the gray stone (on the left) that marks the church's 16th-century expansion. The gray-and-red house above the spire is the **elementary school** (about 25 children attend). Older students go to the "big city," La Spezia. The red building on the hill to the right of the schoolhouse, a former monastery, is now the **City Hall.** Vernazza and neighboring Corniglia function as one community. Through most of the 1990s, the local government was Communist. In 1999, residents elected a coalition of many parties working to rise above ideologies and simply make Vernazza a better place. That practical notion of government continues here today.

Finally, on the top of the hill, with the best view of all, is the **town cemetery.** It's only fair that hardworking Vernazzans—who spend their lives climbing up and down and up and down and up and down the hillsides that hem in their little town—are rewarded with a world-class view from their eternal resting place.

▶ Look high on your right to the castle.

Castle (Castello Doria)

The castle, which is now just stones and a grassy park with super views, still guards the town (€1.50, daily 10:00-20:00, summer until 21:00, closed Nov-March; from harbor, take stairs by Trattoria Gianni and follow *Ristorante al Castello* signs, the tower is a few steps beyond). This was the town's watchtower back in pirate days.

Ristorante Belforte, in the squat tower below the castle overlooking the water, is a great spot for a glass of wine or a meal. From the breakwater, you could follow the rope to the restaurant and pop

The squat Belforte tower (left) and castle tower (right) overlook the sea; both host restaurants.

inside, past an actual submarine door. A photo of a major storm showing the entire tower under a wave (not uncommon in the winter) hangs near the bar.

Harbor

In a moderate storm, you'd get soaked where you're sitting, as waves routinely crash over the *molo* (**breakwater,** built in 1972). Waves can rearrange the huge rocks—depositing them from the breakwater onto the piazza and its benches. Freak waves have even washed away tourists squinting excitedly into their cameras. (I've seen it happen.) In 2007, an American woman was swept away and killed by a rogue wave.

The **train line** (across the harbor) was constructed in 1874 to tie together a newly united Italy, linking Turin and Genoa with Rome. A second line (hidden in a tunnel at this point) was built in the 1920s. The yellow building alongside the tracks was Vernazza's **first train station.** Along the wall behind the tracks, you can see the four bricked-up alcoves where people once waited for trains. The wonderful concrete **sunbathing** strip (and place for late-night privacy) laid below the tracks along the rocks makes for a fun little stroll. (Buoys along the shoreline establish a boat-free swimming zone.)

Vernazza's **fishing fleet** is down to just a few boats with net spools, but Vernazzans are still more likely to own a boat than a car. Boats are moored on buoys, except in winter or when the red storm flag indicates rough seas (see the pole at the start of the breakwater). When the red flag flies, boat owners are permitted to pull them up onto the square—which is usually reserved for restaurant tables. In the 1970s, tiny Vernazza had one of Italy's top water polo teams, and the harbor was their "pool." Later, when the league required a real pool, Vernazza dropped out.

▶ *Stroll from the breakwater to the harbor square. Look for a small historic stone just before the narrow stairway on the right.*

Harbor Square (Piazza Marconi)

Vernazza, with the Cinque Terre's only natural harbor, was established as the sole place boats could pick up the fine local wine. The two-foot-high square **stone** at the foot of the stairs is marked *Sasso del Sego* (stone of tallow). Workers crushed animal flesh and fat in its basin to make tallow, which drained out from the tiny hole below. The tallow was then used to waterproof boats or wine barrels.

Stonework is the soul of the region. Take some time to appreciate the medieval stonework and chestnut timbers of the restaurant interiors facing the harbor. From here steps lead to your right up to the castle.

Towns along this coast were designed as what's called a "Ligurian Palazzata"—an interlinked series of buildings intended to provide protection from seaborne attacks. Vernazza's harborfront retains its thousand-year-old "stockade" of buildings, connected with tiny and

Colorful boats ashore on Vernazza's harbor beach

easy-to-defend staircases leading from the vulnerable harbor higher into the community.

▶ *Cross to the church side of the harbor, and peek into the tiny street leading away from the water with its commotion of arches. Vernazza's most characteristic **side streets** (caruggi) lead up from here. Another narrow set of stairs marks the beginning of the trail that leads up, up, up to the iconic view of Vernazza—and on to Monterosso.*

Vernazza's Church

Vernazza's harborfront church sits on the tiny piazza, decorated with a river-rock mosaic. This popular hangout spot is where the town's older ladies soak up the last bit of sun, and kids enjoy a patch of level ball field. The church, nestled awkwardly into the rocks, is unusual for its east-facing (rather than the standard west-facing) entryway. With relative peace and prosperity in the 16th century, the townspeople doubled the size of their church, extending it west over what was the little piazza that faced it.

Enter under a statue of St. Margaret, patron saint of Vernazza, and climb the steps into the nave. The space was originally dark (with just the upper slit windows) before the bigger gothic windows were added with the 16th-century expansion. The lighter pillars in the back mark the extension. Three historic portable crosses hanging on the walls are carried through town during religious processions. These are replicas of crosses that (locals like to believe) Vernazzan ships once carried on crusades to the Holy Land. The town priest, Don Giovanni, is popular—he stopped the church bells from ringing through the night (light sleepers rejoiced).

Stop by Vernazza's tranquil church...

...and stroll its irresistible main street.

▶ *Now walk back across the harbor square and head left into town. After the lane opens up on the right, hike through the cave to the new beach.*

"New Beach"

This is where the town's stream used to hit the sea back in the 1970s. Older locals remember frolicking on a beach here when they were kids, but the constant, churning surf eventually eroded it all the way back to the cliff. When the 2011 flood hit, it blew out the passageway and deposited landslide material here from the hills above. In the flood's aftermath, Vernazza's main drag and harbor were filled with mud and silt. Workers used the debris to fill in even more of this beach. But as time goes on, the forces of nature are once again taking it away.

▶ *Back on the main drag, continue uphill to...*

Vernazza's "Main Street"

You're now strolling through Vernazza's "commercial center": souvenir shops, wine shops, the Blue Marlin Bar (a good nightspot), and so on. The small stone chapel with iron grillwork over the window (on the right) is the tiny **Chapel of Santa Marta,** where Mass is celebrated on special Sundays. You'll walk by a *gelateria,* bakery, pharmacy, grocery, and another *gelateria.* There are plenty of fun and cheap food-to-go options here. While it's easy to get distracted by all the tourists, try to see through them to notice locals going about their business.

On the right, just before the train tracks, study the big **poster,** which shows photos of the 2011 flood (*alluvione*) and the shops it devastated. "The 25th of October" is a day that will live forever in this town's lore. Vernazza is built around one street—basically a lid over the stream in its ravine. On that fateful day, the surrounding hills acted like a funnel, directing flash-flood waters right through the middle of town. Four townspeople lost their lives. Imagine this street from here to the harbor buried under 13 feet of mud. Every shop, restaurant, and hotel on the main drag had to be rewired, replumbed, and re-equipped.

The second set of train tracks (nearer the harbor) was renovated to lessen disruptive noise. At the base of the stairs a handy monitor displays up-to-the-minute schedules for arriving and departing trains (including any running late—*ritardo*). The walls under the tracks serve as a sort of community information center. Just above the tracks (to the right), the town provides limited space for advertising for political parties (but only during the weeks leading up to an election).

▶ *Hike a few steps under and above the tracks to the little square.*

"Millstone Square"

The **millstones** set on the square are a reminder that the town stream (which goes underground here and which you've been walking over ever since leaving the harbor area) once powered Vernazza's water mill. (You can still see its tiny "river" if you follow this road up a few steps.) Until the 1950s, the river ran openly through the center of town. Old-timers recall the days before the breakwater, when the river cascaded down, charming bridges spanned the ravine, and the surf sent waves rolling up Vernazza's main drag.

Corralling this stream under the modern street, and forcing it to take a hard turn here, contributed to the damage caused by the 2011 flood. After the flood, Swiss engineers redesigned the drainage system, so any future floods will be less destructive. They also installed nets above the town to protect it from landslides.

On the wall ahead at the bend in the road, notice the **World Wars Monument**—dedicated to those killed in World Wars I and II. Not a family in Vernazza was spared.

The **path to Corniglia** begins here (behind and above the monument). Even if you don't plan to hike its entire length, you don't have to go far to find fine views over Vernazza's stony peninsula.

▶ *To see a more workaday part of Vernazza, head a couple of minutes uphill from here to the...*

Top of Town

First you'll pass the **ambulance barn** (on the left, at #7, with big brown garage doors and a *croce verde Vernazza* sign), where a group of volunteers is always on call for a dash to the hospital, 40 minutes away in La Spezia. Farther up, you'll come to a functional strip of modern apartment blocks facing the river. In this practical zone—the only place in town that allows cars—are a bank, the post office, a launderette, and the popular bar/café called Il Pirata delle Cinque Terre. The parking lot fills a square called **Fontana Vecchia,** named for an "old fountain" that's so old, it's long gone. Shuttle buses run from here to hamlets and sanctuaries in the hills above.

Looming over this neighborhood is a terraced hill capped by the town cemetery (a 20-minute steep hike from here), and a 30-minute climb beyond that, the town's Madonna di Reggio sanctuary.

EXPERIENCES IN VERNAZZA

Hikes from Vernazza

For a rundown of ambitious hikes from Vernazza—including the main coastal trail to Corniglia and to Monterosso—see page 26. Here are some alternatives closer to town.

From Vernazza, you can hike in either direction for classic photo ops. Both hikes are steeply, but briefly, uphill (about 10 minutes to the best views and park ticket checkpoints).

For the best light in the morning, follow the trail **toward Corniglia;** you'll twist up through vineyards to earn great views down over the stony back side of Vernazza's peninsula, with its round castle tower poking up and a Monterosso backdrop. The best views are from just before the national park ticket checkpoint. If you need a rewarding rest up here, Bar la Torre offers drinks with a grand view.

The trail **toward Monterosso** has the best light in the evening. From the harbor, you'll hike up through the steep and narrow alleys before popping out on the trail above town. Follow this around the bluff, enjoying better and better views of Vernazza's tidy pastel harbor. The views are fine before the ticket booth, but even better after—if you don't want to buy a Cinque Terre park card, you can hike up here in the evening, after the park officially closes (typically around 19:00).

Hike to the Cemetery: To hike up to Vernazza's sweet little

You can hike uphill from Vernazza (toward Corniglia or Monterosso) for classic views.

cemetery, find the steep lane from the ravine at the top of town. From here, it's a 20-minute hike to the top. You'll find a peaceful world of lovingly tended family graves with stunning views over the Cinque Terre. Imagine the entire village sadly trudging up here during funerals. The cemetery is peaceful and evocative at sunset, when the fading light touches each crypt.

▲▲Madonna di Reggio Shuttle Bus Joyride and/or Hike

For a cheap and scenic joyride (50 minutes, €1.50), with friendly, English-speaking Mirco, Pietro, or Graziella, ride the ATC shuttle bus, which loops about five times a day from the top of Vernazza to sanctuaries and hamlets high in the hills—including the San Bernardino sanctuary and Madonna di Reggio sanctuary—and back (check schedule posted at the bus stop, ask at the TI, or check online at www.atc esercizio.it). Look for the bus to *Madonna di Reggio via Fornacchi*.

Joyride: The bus ride is absolutely stunning. It can be crowded, but most hikers get off at the first stop (San Bernardino). I prefer either to stay on for three-quarters of the loop (to Madonna di Reggio, then hike back to Vernazza; see below), or to stay on to complete the scenic circle.

As you ride, you'll see tiny settlements that predate the Cinque Terre villages, built back when people were afraid to live on the coast for fear of pirates. These hamlets and their terraces go back a thousand years. You'll switchback past chestnut trees, which historically provided wood for fuel and lumber, and chestnuts, which were ground to make a kind of flour in a land with no grain.

Hiking Down from Madonna di Reggio: For a delightful and easy (if steep) half-hour hike into Vernazza, ask the driver to let you out at the stop for *Santuario Nostra Signora di Reggio*.

First, walk two minutes below the bus stop to the sanctuary, which dates from 1248 and has a Romanesque facade. Inside the church, votives (little ships and paintings of ships in angry seas given as tokens of thanks) fill the rear corner—gifts from sailors who survived storms and soldiers who survived wars. A volunteer staffs the church selling coffee, water, and snacks.

From here signs direct you to trail #508—the historic trail down to Vernazza. You'll be walking on thousand-year-old cobbles through abandoned olive groves and past the Stations of the Cross, which have inspired generations of processions trudging up from Vernazza. You

Enjoy Vernazza's "new beach"…   …and the sunning rocks at the harbor.

may see a parked *trenino,* a mini-train that helps farmers get their grapes from distant fields to their trucks.

You'll descend through the cemetery, then either take the stairs down to the train station, or continue to the left down the lane to the square called Fontana Vecchia, where you caught the shuttle bus.

Beaches

The harbor's sandy cove has sunning rocks and showers by the breakwater. The sunbathing lane directly under the church has a shower. A ladder on the sea side of the breakwater aids deep-water swimmers. And, while it's getting smaller and rockier each year, Vernazza's "new beach" can be accessed through a hole halfway along the town's main drag.

Boat Rides

In addition to the regularly scheduled big boats that depart from Vernazza's harbor (see page 16), hiring your own boat can be handy for intertown transport. It's also a great way to escape the crowds and get a different angle on Cinque Terre splendor. From Vernazza, figure around €50 one-way to boat to the other towns (for up to six passengers in an outboard). Or hire a boat for a one-hour sightseeing cruise of the entire Cinque Terre (about €150); one popular stop is the tiny *acqua pendente* (waterfall) cove between Vernazza and Monterosso, which locals call their *laguna blu.*

Some boat captains offer evening *aperitivo* cruises. At Vernazza's breakwater you'll find **Nord Est,** run by Vincenzo (with help from Cesare), the best-established option (mobile 338-700-0436, info@

Vernazza's breakwater offers a shimmering view of the harbor at night.

nordest-vernazza.com). **Vernazza Water Taxi,** run by Pietro, is another choice (mobile 338-911-3869, info@vernazzawatertaxi.it).

Wine Tasting

Vernazza Wine Experience hides out at the top of town just under the castle. Run by Alessandro, a sommelier, it's romantic, with mellow music and a hardwood, ship-deck ambience. Tastings start at €15/person and can be matched up with meat-and-cheese small plates. While the bill can add up, the quality is excellent and the view is unforgettable (cash only, daily 17:00-20:00, hike from harborfront and turn left before castle, Via S. Giovanni Battista 31, tel. 331-343-3801). Or, drop by his place behind the train station called **Cinque Sensi** (similar prices, Via Roma 71, daily 12:00-24:00).

A Little Taste of Opera

A favorite Cinque Terre evening memory for many is Vernazza's summer opera. A big-name maestro from Lucca brings talented singers to town twice weekly. Performances (two singers and a piano) fill the small oratory, a medieval building with fine acoustics that was beautifully restored for this purpose (just up the steps from the church).

Performances begin at 19:00 and last just over an hour—strategically timed to squeeze between a late-afternoon aperitivo on the harbor and a 20:30 dinner reservation (€18 in advance, €20 at the door, May-Oct Wed and Fri at 19:00, book tickets at Cinque Terre Riviera office at #24 on the main street, tel. 0187-812-123, info@cinqueterreriviera.com).

NIGHTLIFE IN VERNAZZA

Vernazza generally shuts down pretty early. The town's nightlife centers on the bars on its waterfront piazza, which is the place to "see and be seen." Young restaurant workers work hard throughout the tourist season, but they let loose after-hours and enjoy connecting with international visitors in the town's few nightspots (which are required to close by midnight). For a more genteel option, consider an opera performance or a wine tasting (both described earlier). Or in the cool, calm evening, sit on the town's breakwater with a glass of wine and watch the phosphorescence in the waves.

The **Blue Marlin Bar** dominates the late-night scene with a mix of locals and tourists, good drinks, and an open piano. If you play piano, you're welcome to join in. **Ananasso Bar** offers early-evening happy-hour fun and cocktails (*aperitivi*) that both locals and visitors enjoy. Its harborfront tables get the last sunshine of the day. For more on these bars, see their listings under "Eating in Vernazza," later.

SLEEPING IN VERNAZZA

Vernazza lacks any real hotels, and almost all of my listings are *affitta-camere* (private rooms for rent). I favor hosts who rent multiple rooms and have a proven track record of good communication (they speak just enough English, have email, and are reliable). Airbnb is really big in Vernazza.

Most places accept only cash, promise free Wi-Fi (often spotty), and don't include breakfast unless noted. Some have killer views, and some come with lots of stairs. Expect noise at night: Trains tearing through, church bells (after 7:00 and before 22:00), crashing waves, cars in the upper town. Come to think of it, just pack earplugs.

While a few places have all their beds in one building, most have rooms scattered all over town. Better-organized outfits have an informal reception desk (sometimes at a restaurant or other business) where you can check in. But many places have no reception at all. (The Vernazza map in this book shows only the places that have a fixed address or reception office; if I mention "reception," you'll check in there.)

If you overnight here, communicate your arrival time to your host and get clear instructions on where to meet and pick up the keys. They'll usually offer to meet you at the train station if they know when you're coming.

Rooms For Rent *(Affittacamere)*

The **Cinque Terre Riviera** agency, based in Vernazza, rents rooms here and throughout the region (www.cinqueterreriviera.com; see page 55).

Scattered Through the Town Center

More Expensive, with More Amenities

$$$$ La Malà is the town's jet-setter pad. Four crisp, pristine white rooms boast fancy-hotel-type extras and a shared seaview terrace. It's a climb—way up to the top of town—but they'll carry your bags to and from the station. Book early; this place fills up quickly (includes breakfast at a bar, family rooms, air-con, mobile 334-287-5718, www.lamala. it, info@lamala.it, charming Giamba and his mama, Armanda). They also rent two rooms at the simpler **$ "Armanda's Room"** nearby—a great value, since you get Giamba's attention to detail and amenities without paying for a big view (includes simple breakfast, air-con).

$$$$ Vernazza sul Mare rents two view, luxury apartments (one- and two-bedroom, sleeping 4-6) that overlook the sea and town from private, spacious terraces. The light-filled, airy units come with sea breezes and a crashing-waves soundtrack. These are great for families and can be connected for larger groups (both with air-con, fully equipped kitchens, climb steps up to Via Carattino 12, mobile 345-363-6118, www.vernazzasulmare.com, info@vernazzasulmare.com, run by helpful American-Italian Ruth and her family).

$$$ Nicolina Rooms consists of seven rooms and one apartment in three buildings. Two cheaper rooms are in the center over the pharmacy, up a few steep steps; another, pricier studio with a terrace is on a twisty lane above the harbor; and four more rooms are in a building beyond the church, with great views and church bells (all include breakfast, Piazza Marconi 29—check in at Pizzeria Vulnetia, tel. 0187-821-193, mobile 333-842-6879, www.camerenicolina.it, info@camerenicolina.it).

$$$ La Marina Rooms is run by hardworking Christian, who speaks English and happily meets guests at the station to carry bags. There are five well-tended, airy, and renovated units, most high above the main street: One single works as a (very) tight double, and three doubles have fine oceanview terraces; he also has two apartments—one with terrace and sea views, and the other on the harborfront square (rooms have fridges, mobile 338-476-7472, www.lamarina rooms.com, mapcri@yahoo.it).

$$$ Monica Lercari rents several rooms with modern comforts, perched at the top of town (more for seaview terrace, includes breakfast, air-con, tel. 0187-812-296, mobile 320-025-4515, monimarimax@gmail.com). Monica and her husband, Massimo, run the recommended Ristorante al Castello, in the old castle tower overlooking town.

Simpler, Good-Value Places

$$ Francamaria and her husband Andrea rent 10 sharp, comfortable, and creatively renovated rooms. Their reception desk is on the harbor square (on the ground floor at Piazza Marconi 30), but the rooms they manage are all over town (family rooms, some with air-con, mobile 328-711-9728, www.francamaria.com, francamariareservation@gmail.com). They also rent a room in Manarola.

$$ Emanuela Colombo rents a spacious and classy room on the harbor square, and a molto chic split-level apartment on a quiet side street (sleeps up to four, reception at Via Roma 27, tel. 339-834-2486, www.vacanzemanuela.it, manucap64@libero.it).

$$ Vernazza Rooms, run by Massimo, rents 14 rooms: Four are above the Blue Marlin Bar looking down on the main street, and seven are a steep climb higher up, just under the City Hall (big family apartments, a few with air-con and others with fans, fridges in all rooms, arrange check-in time in advance and meet your host at Via del Santo 9, mobile 351-918-3164, www.vernazzarooms.com, info@vernazza rooms.com).

$$ Lovely **Rosa Vitali** rents a four-person apartment with a full kitchen; it's across from the pharmacy overlooking the main street—and beyond the train noise (ring bell at Via Visconti 10—just before the tobacco shop near Piazza Marconi, tel. 0187-821-181, mobile 340-267-5009, www.rosacamere.it, rosa.vitali@libero.it).

$$ Maria Capellini rents two simple, clean rooms that face each other across the harbor; one is at ground level just steps from the beach and with a view; the other looks over a skinny street (fridge, fans, mobile 338-436-3411, www.mariacapellini.com, mariacapellini@hotmail.it, kindly Maria and Giacomo).

$$ Martina Callo's four old-fashioned, spartan rooms overlook the harbor square; they're up plenty of steps near the silent-at-night church tower. While the rooms are simple, guests pay for and appreciate the views (family rooms, cheaper no-view room, air-con, ring bell at Piazza Marconi 26, tel. 0187-812-365, mobile 329-435-5344, www.roomartina.it, roomartina@roomartina.it), Martina and her father, Giuseppe.

$ Rooms Francesca offers one tidy room with sea views and air-con, and a two-bedroom apartment with fans. Both hide out in the steep streets just below City Hall (check in at Enoteca Sciacchetrà at Via Roma 19, tel. 0187-821-112, mobile 339-101-2962, www.5terre-vernazza.it, moggia.franco@libero.it; Francesca, Franco, and Sabine).

$ Ivo's Camere rents two tight but well-appointed rooms several flights of stairs above the main street (air-con, Via Roma 6, mobile 333-477-5521, www.ivocamere.com, post@ivocamere.com).

$ Albergo Barbara rents nine tidy, Ikea-chic top-floor rooms overlooking the square with a communal attic lounge. Most have small windows and small views; view rooms are more expensive. It's a good value in a nice location, run by Alessio and Alberto (cheaper rooms with shared bathroom, lots of stairs, reserve online with credit card but pay cash, Piazza Marconi 30, tel. 0187-812-398, www.albergobarbara.it, info@albergobarbara.it).

$ Memo Rooms rents two clean and spacious rooms overlooking the main street, in what feels like a miniature hotel. Enrica will meet you if you call upon arrival (Via Roma 15, try Enrica's mobile first at 338-285-2385, otherwise call 0187-812-360, www.memorooms.com, info@memorooms.com).

More Options

If my recommendations above are full, try these:

$$ Capitano Rooms (3 rooms and 1 apartment several flights of stairs above main drag, fans; ask for Julia, Paolo, Edoardo, or Barbara at

Trattoria del Capitano restaurant on main square at Piazza Marconi 21, tel. 0187-812-201, www.tavernavernazza.com, info@tavernavernazza. com); **$ Eva's Rooms** (2 rooms on main street, air-con, train noise, 2-night minimum, call ahead to arrange meeting place, tel. 334-798-6500, www.evasrooms.it, evasrooms@yahoo.it); **$$$ Rooms Elisabetta** (2 tight, renovated, casually run rooms and 1 apartment at the tip-top of town with Vernazza's ultimate 360-degree roof terrace—come here for the views; fans, partway up Corniglia path at Via Carattino 62, mobile 347-451-1834, www.elisabettacarro.com, carro-elisabetta@hotmail.com, Elisabetta); **$$ Manuela Moggia** (3 apartments and 2 rooms, more for kitchen or view, behind train station at Via Gavino 22 and on main square, tel. 0187-812-397, mobile 333-413-6374, www.manuela-vernazza.com, info@manuela-vernazza.com).

In the Inland Part of Town

Above the Train Station: $$$$ Casa Cato offers six modern, tight but well-outfitted rooms, some with private balconies and all with access to an inviting shared terrace overlooking the sea and town (RS%, air-con, fridge, expect some train noise, mobile 334-123-8579, www. casacatocinqueterre.com, info@casacatocinqueterre.com, Lisa). They also rent an apartment in the center of town.

$$$ Giuliano Basso's four carefully crafted, well-appointed rooms form a cozy little compound with a common lounge and view terrace, straddling a ravine among orange trees. Giuliano—the town's last stone-layer—proudly built the place himself. To reach this quiet retreat on the green hillside just above town and the train station, you'll climb partway up the Corniglia footpath (2 rooms have air-con, more train noise than others; follow the main road up above the station, take the ramp up toward Corniglia just before Pensione Sorriso, follow the path, and watch for a sharp left turn—or ask Giuliano to meet you at the station; mobile 333-341-4792, www.cameregiuliano. com, giuliano@cdh.it).

In the Ravine at the Top of Town: These practical options are a five-minute, gently uphill stroll behind the train station. While this functional zone is less atmospheric, it is easy to access (with fewer steep stairs). There's no train or church-bell noise—the constant soundtrack is Vernazza's gurgling river—but there can be traffic noise.

$$ Camere Fontanavecchia, run by Annamaria, is the best choice here, with eight bright and cheery rooms (three with terraces) overlooking the ravine and its rushing river (Via Gavino 15, tel. 0187-821-130, mobile 333-454-9371, www.cinqueterrecamere.com, m.annamaria@libero.it). She also rents an apartment.

$$ Tonino Basso/La Perla, spread over two floors, has 10 over-priced rooms in a drab, elevator-equipped, modern apartment block. La Perla's rooms feel fresher (air-con, fridge, Via Gavino 34, mobile 339-761-1651, www.toninobasso.com and www.laperladelle5terre.it, Alessandra).

$ La Rosa dei Venti ("The Compass Rose"), run by Giuliana Basso, houses three airy, good-value rooms in her childhood home, on the third floor of an apartment building (call to arrange meeting time, air-con, Via Gavino 19, mobile 333-762-4679, www.larosadeiventi-vernazza.it, info@larosadeiventi-vernazza.it).

Guesthouse (*Pensione*)

$$$ Gianni Franzi, a busy restaurant on the harbor square, runs the closest thing to a big hotel in Vernazza. There are 25 small rooms scattered across three buildings a hundred tight, winding stairs above the harbor square. Some rooms (including a few cheaper ones with shared bathrooms) are funky and decorated à la shipwreck, with tiny balconies and grand sea views. The comfy, newer rooms lack views. All guests have access to a super-scenic cliff-hanging garden and panoramic terrace (where breakfast is served in season). Steely Marisa requires check-in before 16:00 or a phone call to explain when you're coming. Emanuele, Simona, and staff speak enough English (RS%, closed Jan-Feb, Piazza Marconi 1, tel. 0187-812-228, mobile 393-900-8155, www.giannifranzi.it, info@giannifranzi.it). Pick up your keys at the restaurant, but on Wed, when the restaurant is closed, call ahead to make other arrangements.

EATING IN VERNAZZA

Breakfast

Vernazza has plenty of options, from full bacon and eggs (Blue Marlin and Capitano), to a Sicilian bakery of fresh pastries (Il Pirata), to coffee and a sweet roll on the harborfront (Ananasso), to any number of bakeries selling sweet and savory options to go. For a full breakfast,

Twin brothers run the popular Il Pirata delle Cinque Terre café.

you'll pay €12-15. Here are your main options from the top of town to the harbor.

$ Il Pirata delle Cinque Terre, at the parking lot at the top of town, is playful, efficient, comfortable, and serves tasty breakfast bruschetta, frittatas, and an array of fresh pastries. The fun service of the dynamic duo Gianluca and Massimo (hardworking Sicilian twins, a.k.a. the Cannoli brothers) makes up for the lack of a view. They pride themselves on not serving bacon and eggs, since "this is Italy" (daily 7:00-24:00, also serves lunch and dinner—see later, Via Gavino 36, tel. 0187-812-047).

$$ Blue Marlin Bar (midtown, just below the train station) serves a good array of clearly priced à la carte breakfast items (Italian breakfast from 7:30, eggs and bacon 8:30-11:30). If you're awaiting a train and the platform isn't crowded, it's pleasant to have a drink at Blue Marlin's outdoor seating in view of the tracks (Thu-Tue 7:30-23:00, closed Wed).

$ Lunch Box is the hardworking new kid on the block, with lots of hot options and a fun little perch for a couple of tables overlooking the main drag (daily 7:00-22:00, also serves lunch and dinner—see later, Via Roma 34, mobile 338-908-2841, Stefano).

$$ **Trattoria del Capitano** offers outdoor seating on the harbor, as well as cozy spots inside the restaurant and a full menu (Wed-Mon 8:00-22:00, closed Tue except in Aug, on Piazza Marconi, tel. 0187-812-201, hardworking Paolo and Barbara speak English).

$$ **Ananasso Bar** has a youthful energy, a great location right on the harbor, and a skimpy Italian breakfast menu (toasted *panini,* pastries, muesli with yogurt, and cappuccino). You can eat a bit cheaper at the bar (you're welcome to picnic on the nearby bench or seawall rocks with a sea view) or enjoy the best-situated tables in town (Fri-Wed 8:00-late, closed Thu, on Piazza Marconi).

Picnic Breakfast: Drop by one of Vernazza's many little bakeries, focaccia shops, or grocery stores to assemble a breakfast to eat on the breakwater. Top it off with a coffee in a nearby bar.

Lunch and Dinner

Vernazza's restaurants work hard to win your business. Wander around at about 20:00 and compare the ambience. If you dine in Vernazza but are staying in another town, check train schedules before sitting down to eat, as evening trains run less frequently, with gaps in the schedule. To get an outdoor table on summer weekends, reserve ahead. Harborside restaurants and bars are easygoing. You're welcome to grab a cup of coffee or glass of wine and disappear somewhere on the breakwater, returning your glass when you're done. You've got lots of options and prices are competitive, with €11-15 pastas and €15-25 *secondi.*

Harborside

$$$ **Gianni Franzi** is an old standby for well-prepared seafood and pastas. Emanuele, Nicolas, and their crew provide steady, reliable, and friendly service. The outdoor seating is partially tucked under an arcade, while the indoor setting is big, open, and classy (check their *menù cucina tipica Vernazza,* Thu-Tue 12:00-15:00 & 19:00-22:00, closed Wed except in Aug, tel. 0187-812-228).

$$$ **Trattoria del Capitano** feels unpretentious and serves a short menu of straightforward local dishes, including *spaghetti allo scoglio*—pasta entangled with various types of seafood (for hours and location, see "Breakfast," earlier).

$$$ Ristorante Pizzeria Vulnetia has a nautical, jovial atmosphere. It serves regional specialties; but unlike the others, it also dishes up thin-crust pizzas—making this a good choice for a group with differing tastes, those on a budget, and families (Tue-Sun 12:00-22:00, closed Mon, Piazza Marconi 29, tel. 0187-821-193, Tullio and Federica).

$$ Pizzeria Baia Saracena ("Saracen Bay") serves forgettable pizza and pasta out on the breakwater. Eat here not for high cuisine, but for a memorable atmosphere at reasonable prices (Sat-Thu 11:30-22:00, closed Fri, tel. 0187-812-113, Luca and Andrea).

$$$$ Gambero Rosso rounds out the options on the harbor. Long the top restaurant in town, today it's lost its edge (it was sold to a big-city restaurateur who runs it from afar). Still, it's reliably good, and has a fine interior and great outdoor tables (Fri-Wed 12:00-15:00 & 19:00-22:00, closed Thu and Dec-Feb, Piazza Marconi 7, tel. 0187-812-265).

Above the Harbor, by the Castle

$$$$ Ristorante Belforte is a cut above the rest, serving a fine blend of traditional and creative cuisine, fishy *spaghetti alla Bruno, trofie al pesto* (hand-rolled noodles with pesto), and classic *antipasto misto di pesce*—an assortment of fish (€24/person for 5 plates; 2-person minimum). From the breakwater, a rope leads up from the harbor to a web of tables embedded in four levels of the old castle. While their indoor seating is great, for the ultimate seaside perch, reserve a table on the *terrazza con vista* (view terrace) or request the "lovers' table" on its own little terrace. Most of Belforte's seating is outdoors—if the weather's bad, the interior can get crowded. Late in the evening, Andrea cranks up the fun (Wed-Mon 12:00-15:00 & 19:00-22:00, closed Tue and Nov-March, tel. 0187-812-222, Michela).

$$$ Ristorante al Castello—a bit less expensive and a bit more homey than the others—is run by gracious and English-speaking Monica, her husband Massimo, and their sometimes-gruff staff. Hike high above town to just below the castle for commanding views. Reserve one of the dozen romantic cliffside seaview tables for two—some of the tables snake around the castle, where you'll feel like you're eating all alone with the Mediterranean. Monica offers a free *sciacchetrà* or *limoncello* and biscotti with this book by request

(Thu–Tue 12:00–15:00 & 19:00–22:00, closed Wed and Nov–April, tel. 0187-812-296).

On or near the Main Street

Several of Vernazza's inland eateries manage to compete without the harbor ambience but with slightly cheaper prices.

$$ Trattoria da Sandro, on the main drag, mixes quality Genovese and Ligurian cuisine with friendly service and can be a peaceful alternative to the harborside scene. The family proudly maintains its cultural traditions and dishes up award-winning stuffed mussels (Wed-Mon 12:00-15:00 & 18:30-22:00, closed Tue, Via Roma 62, tel. 0187-812-223, Argentina and Alessandro).

$$ Antica Osteria il Baretto is another solid bet for homey, reasonably priced traditional cuisine, run by Simone and Jenny. As it's off the harbor and less glitzy than the others, it's favored by locals who prefer less noisy English while they eat great homemade fare. Sitting deep in their interior can be a tranquil escape (Tue-Sun 12:00-22:00, closed Mon, indoor and outdoor seating in summer, Via Roma 31, tel. 0187-812-381).

Other Eating Options

$$ Blue Marlin Bar, on the main street, busts out of the Vernazzan cuisine rut with a short, creative menu of more casual dishes (pizzas, salads). It's a good choice if you want to grab something basic rather than dine (for more details and hours, see "Breakfast," earlier).

$$ Il Pirata delle Cinque Terre, a huge hit for breakfast, also attracts travelers for lunch and dinner. While you're eating at the parking lot, the food, service, and energy are great. And many are charmed by the Cannoli twins, who entertain while they serve. The menu (pastas and salads) is aimed squarely at American tourists' taste buds (lunch from 12:00, reserve ahead for dinner from 18:00, good cannoli and Sicilian slushies, at the top of town; for more details and contact info, see "Breakfast," earlier). The self-serve laundry is next door for those who like to multitask.

$ Lunch Box serves *panini,* salads, and fresh fruit juices from a clever and flexible menu. Assemble your own salad (or juice) from a long list of ingredients (for hours and location, see "Breakfast," earlier).

$ Pizzeria Ercole dishes out an array of fried and greasy gut-bombs cheap and fast with tables right in the busy center of town. More tables are in a humble little secret terrace hiding in the back (where tour guides go to escape the crowds). You're welcome to sit and munch for their takeaway prices (daily, Via Visconti 2, tel. 0187-812-545).

Pizzerias, Sandwiches, and Groceries: Vernazza's main-street eateries offer a fine range of quick meals. Several bakeries and creative little takeaway joints sell sandwiches and pizza by the slice. **Pino's grocery store** at #19 makes inexpensive sandwiches to order (generally Mon-Sat 8:00-13:00 & 17:00-19:30, closed Sun).

Gelato: The town has plenty of good gelato shops. On the harbor, the aptly named **Gelateria Il Porticciolo** ("Marina") uses fresh ingredients to create intense flavors (try their *cannella*—cinnamon, or *nocciola*—hazelnut). **Gelateria Vernazza,** near the top of the main street, takes its gelato seriously, occasionally flirting with creative ingredients (soy) and flavors (*riso*—rice, and ricotta and fig). **Gelateria Amore Mio** (midtown) used to be Gelateria Stalin, founded in 1968 by a pastry chef with that unfortunate name; now it's run by his niece Sonia and nephew Francesco, with great people-watching tables.

Corniglia

If you think of the Cinque Terre as The Beatles, Corniglia is Ringo. This tiny, sleepy town is the only one of the five not directly on the water. According to legend, the town was originally settled by a Roman farmer who named it for his mother, Cornelia (which is how Corniglia is pronounced). Locals claim that its ancient residents produced a wine so widely exported that vases have been found at Pompeii stamped with the town name. Wine remains Corniglia's lifeblood today. Sample some when you're in town.

Less visited than the other Cinque Terre towns, Corniglia has fewer tourists, cooler temperatures, a laid-back main square, a few restaurants, a windy overlook on its promontory, and plenty of private rooms for rent. You don't go to Corniglia for the beach: Its once fine beach below the station has washed away. From the town center, signs for *al mare* or *Marina* point to where a stepped path leads steeply down to sunning rocks.

ORIENTATION TO CORNIGLIA

Hill-capping Corniglia is connected with its train station far below by a long set of stairs, and much easier, by a hardworking little shuttle bus. Its reliable schedule is posted both at the station and in the town. Because of the steep distance between the town and its station, and the lack of a boat dock, Corniglia is inconvenient as a home base for town-hopping.

Tourist Information

A TI/park information office is at the train station (likely daily 8:00-20:00, shorter hours off-season). At busy times, there may also be a kiosk up in town on Ciappà square.

Arrival in Corniglia

By Train: From the station far below town, you can take a footpath zigzagging up 385 steps to the town in about 20 minutes. Or hop on the tiny ATC shuttle that connects the station with Corniglia's main square, where my short self-guided walk starts (buy bus ticket at station TI, €1.50—more from driver, 2-4/hour, generally timed to meet arriving trains, bus departs when full).

Nearly 400 steps link Corniglia's town (above) to its train station (below).

1 Villa Cecio Rooms
2 Pan e Vin Bar
(Ricci Rooms Check-In)
3 Il Carugio Rooms
& Butiega Gastronomia
4 Corniglia Hostel
5 Ristorante il Buongustaio
6 Osteria Mananan &
Enoteca il Pirùn
7 La Posada Ristorante
8 Gelateria

If leaving Corniglia by train, review the shuttle schedule to plan your return to the station.

By Car: Only residents can park on the main road between the recommended Villa Cecio and the point where the steep switchback staircase meets the road. Beyond that area, anyone can park for a fee. All parking areas are within an easy and fairly level walk of the town center.

CORNIGLIA WALK

We'll explore this tiny town—population 240—and end at a scenic viewpoint. This self-guided walk might take 30 minutes or more...but only if you let yourself browse, sample the wine, or lick a gelato cone.

▶ Begin near the shuttle-bus stop located at a...

Town Square
The gateway to this community is Ciappà square, with an ATM, old

wine press, bus stop, and sometimes a TI kiosk in summer. The Cinque Terre's designation as a national park sparked a revitalization of the town.

▶ *Look for the arrow pointing to the centro. Stroll along Via Fieschi, the spine of Corniglia. In the fall, the smell of grapes (on their way to becoming wine) wafts from busy cellars. Along this main street, you'll see...*

Corniglia's Enticing Shops

As you enter Via Fieschi, a trio of neighboring gelato shops jockeys for your business. My favorite is the last one you come to (at #74, on the right), **Alberto's Gelateria** (open late). Before ordering, get a free taste of Alberto's *miele di Corniglia,* made from local honey; he and Cristina are also proud of their basil flavor. Their lemon slush (*granita*) takes pucker to new heights.

Farther along, on the left, **Enoteca il Pirùn**—named for a type of oddly shaped old-fashioned wine pitcher designed to aerate the wine and give the alcohol more kick as you squirt it into your mouth—is located in a cool cantina at Via Fieschi 115. Try some local wines (small tastes generally free, €3/glass). If you order wine to drink from the *pirùn,* Mario will give you a bib. While this is a practicality (rookies tend to dribble), it also makes a nice souvenir.

Farther along, **Butiega Gastronomia** (#142) is an old-fashioned grocery store/deli where Vincenzo sells organic local specialties (daily 8:00-19:30). For picnickers, they offer €5 made-to-order ham-and-cheese sandwiches and a fun *antipasti misti* (priced by weight). Veronica prepares specialties such as pesto daily in the shop's tiny kitchen. You'll find good places to picnic farther along on this walk.

▶ *Following Via Fieschi, you'll end up at the mellow...*

Corniglia's lanes offer slice-of-life scenes...

...and enticing, authentic shops.

Main Square (Largo Taragio)

On the main square, tables from two bars and a trattoria spill around a WWI memorial and the town's old well. It once piped in natural spring water from the hillside to locals living without plumbing. What looks like a church is the **Oratory of Santa Caterina.** (An oratory is a kind of spiritual clubhouse for a service group doing social work in the name of the Catholic Church.) Up the stairs and behind the oratory, you'll find a terrace that children have made into a soccer field. The stone benches and viewpoint make this a peaceful place for a picnic (less crowded than the end-of-town viewpoint, described next).

▶ *Opposite the oratory, notice how steps lead steeply down (in 5 minutes) on Via alla Marina to sunning rocks and a small deck (with a shower and treacherous entry into the water). From the square, continue up Via Fieschi to the...*

End-of-Town Viewpoint

The Santa Maria Belvedere, named for a church that once stood here, marks the scenic end of Corniglia. This is a super picnic spot. From here, look high to the west (right), where the village and sanctuary of San Bernardino straddle a ridge (accessible by shuttle bus or a long uphill hike from Vernazza). Way down below are the local swimming hole and huge sunning rocks.

EXPERIENCES IN CORNIGLIA

Hikes from Corniglia

From town, you can hike on the coastal trail to **Vernazza.** Also consider the challenging but rewarding "high road" to **Manarola via Volastra.** For details, see "Hiking the Cinque Terre" on page 20.

SLEEPING IN CORNIGLIA

Because Corniglia has no harbor, its mostly humble accommodations are almost never full.

$$ Villa Cecio (pronounced "chay-choh"), sits atop the old-time Ristorante Cecio (with great views). They offer eight freshly decorated, well-priced, sizeable rooms on the quiet outskirts of town. Most

rooms have postcard views, and three have terraces—worth requesting when you book. All rooms share a big rooftop view terrace (breakfast extra, four rooms have air-con, on main road toward Vernazza at Via Serra 58—keep going 200 yards beyond Ciappà square and you'll find it on the right, tel. 0187-812-043, mobile 366-285-1178, www.cecio5terre.com, info@cecio5terre.com, Giacinto). They also rent eight more rooms in an annex on the square where the bus stops.

$ Cristiana Ricci communicates well and is reliable, renting three small, clean, and peaceful rooms—one with a terrace and sweeping view—just inland from the bus stop (family rooms, check in at Pan e Vin bar at Via Fieschi 123, mobile 338-937-6547, www.corniglia-room.com, cri_affittacamere@virgilio.it). She also rents three big, modern apartments.

$ Il Carugio has nine modern, fresh, sunny rooms in three buildings—some in the center of the village, and most with sea views. The main building offers a communal rooftop terrace with a commanding view of the coast (2-night minimum, family rooms, air-con, no breakfast but small self-service kitchen, free parking, free self-serve laundry, tel. 0187-812-293, mobile 335-175-7946 or 339-228-3803, www.

ilcarugiodicorniglia.com, info@ilcarugiodicorniglia.com, gregarious Lidia). They also have a two-bedroom apartment facing the main
square.

¢ **Corniglia Hostel,** the town's former schoolhouse, rents 24 beds
in a yellow municipal building up some steps from the square where
the bus stops (find the entrance at the back of the building). Despite
its institutional atmosphere, the hostel's prices, central location, and
bright, clean rooms ensure its popularity. Its hotelesque double rooms
are open to anyone (breakfast extra, office open 7:00-13:00 & 15:00-
1:30 in the morning, air-con, self-serve laundry, Via alla Stazione 3,
tel. 0187-812-559, www.ostellocorniglia.com, ostellocorniglia@gmail.
com, Andrea, Alessandro, and Elisabetta).

EATING IN CORNIGLIA

A typical array of pizzerias, *focaccerie,* and *alimentari* (grocery stores)
line the narrow main drag. I've highlighted a few places for a quick
bite on my self-guided walk, earlier.

For a full, sit-down meal, consider one of these restaurants.

$$$ Ristorante il Buongustaio is a good bet for dinner on the
square. Daniela and the Guelfi family pride themselves in serving
cucina casalinga (home cooking) and good seafood pasta and risotto
(nice tables on the main square as well as in a big indoor dining room,
daily 12:00-21:15, Via Fieschi 164, tel. 0187-821-424).

$$ Osteria Mananan—between the Ciappà bus stop and the
main square at Via Fieschi 117—has earned a good reputation with
tasty dishes and a small, stony, elegant interior (Tue-Sun 12:30-14:30
& 19:30-22:00, closed Mon, no outdoor seating, tel. 0187-821-166).

$$ Enoteca il Pirùn, on Via Fieschi, has a small restaurant above
the wine bar, where Mario serves typical local dishes (Fri-Wed 12:00-
16:00 & 19:00-23:30, closed Thu, tel. 0187-812-315).

$$ La Posada Ristorante offers dinner in a garden under trees,
overlooking the Ligurian Sea. To get here, stroll out of town to the top
of the stairs that lead down to the station (daily 12:00-16:00 & 19:00-
23:00, closed Nov-March, tel. 0187-821-174, mobile 338-232-5734).

Manarola

Mellow Manarola fills a ravine, bookended by its wild little harbor to the west and a diminutive hilltop church square inland to the east. Manarola is exceptional for being unexceptional: While Vernazza is prettier, Monterosso glitzier, Riomaggiore bigger, and Corniglia more rustic, Manarola hits a fine balance, giving it the "just right" combination of Cinque Terre qualities. Perhaps that's why it's a favorite among savvy Europeans seeking a relatively untrampled home base.

Manarola, whose hillsides are blanketed with vineyards, also provides the easiest access to the Cinque Terre's remarkable dry-stone terraces. The trail ringing the town's cemetery peninsula, adjacent to the main harbor, provides some of the most strikingly beautiful town views anywhere in the region.

ORIENTATION TO MANAROLA

The touristy zone squeezed between the cement-encased train tracks and the harbor can be stressfully congested, but head just a few steps uphill and you can breathe again. For a look at all the facets of this delightful town, follow my gentle self-guided stroll from the harbor up through town to the vineyards, and a stunning Mediterranean viewpoint.

Tourist Information

The TI/national park information office is in the train station (likely daily 8:00-20:00, shorter hours off-season).

Arrival in Manarola

By Train: To reach Manarola from the train station, you'll walk through a 200-yard-long tunnel that's lined with interesting photos. (During WWII air raids, these tunnels provided refuge and a safe place for rattled villagers to sleep.) To reach the busy harbor—with touristy restaurants, a boat dock, and the start of my self-guided walk—head left (downhill) when you come out of the tunnel.

The ATC **shuttle bus** runs from near the old waterwheel (halfway up Manarola's main street), stopping first at the parking lots above town, and then going all the way up to Volastra (about 2/hour except for afternoon breaks).

By Car: You're better off parking in La Spezia. If you're overnighting here, ask your hotelier for parking advice. Park your car in one of the two pay lots just before town, then walk down the road to the church; from there, it's an easy downhill walk to the main piazza, train-station tunnel, and harbor (the start of my self-guided walk), or you can wait for the shuttle bus.

Manarola has picturesque perches...   ...and an artsy square.

MANAROLA WALK

From the harbor, this 45-minute self-guided walk shows you the town and surrounding vineyards and ends at a fantastic viewpoint.

▶ *Start down at the waterfront. Belly up to the wooden banister overlooking the rocky harbor, between the two restaurants.*

Harbor

Manarola is tiny and picturesque, a tumble of buildings bunny-hopping down its ravine to the fun-loving waterfront. The **breakwater**—which attempts to make this jagged harbor a bit less dangerous—was built (with reject marble from Carrara) just over a decade ago. Notice how the I-beam crane launches the boats (which must be pulled ashore when bad weather is expected, to avoid being smashed or swept away).

Facing the water, look up to the right, at the hillside Punta Bonfiglio **cemetery** and park. The trail running around the base of the point—where this walk ends—offers magnificent views back on this part of town.

The town's **swimming hole** is just below you. Manarola has no sand, but offers the best deep-water swimming in the area. The first "beach" has a shower, ladder, and wonderful rocks. The second has tougher access and no shower, but feels more remote and pristine (follow the paved path toward Corniglia, just around the point).

▶ *Go inland up the town's main drag—you'll climb a steep ramp to Manarola's "new" square, which covers the train tracks.*

Piazza Capellini

Built in 2004, this square is an all-around great idea, giving the town a safe, fun zone for kids. Locals living near the tracks also enjoy a little less train noise. The mosaic in the middle of the square depicts the varieties of local fish in colorful enamel.

▶ *Go down the stairs at the upper end of the square. On your right, notice the tunnel that leads to Manarola's train station (and the closed Via dell'Amore trailhead). Head up...*

Via Discovolo

Manarola's main street twists up through town, lined by modest shops and filled with pooped hikers. About 100 yards up, just before the

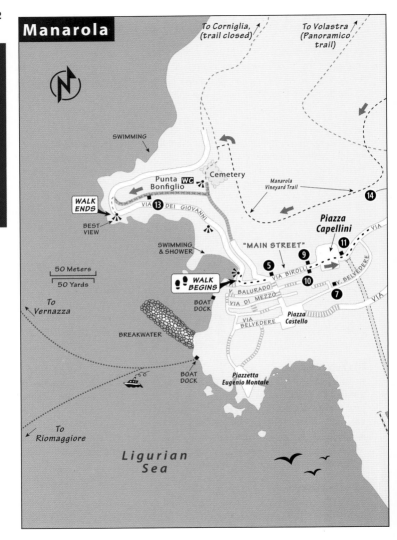

Manarola

To Corniglia,
(trail closed)

To Volastra
(Panoramico
trail)

SWIMMING

Punta
Bonfiglio **WC** Cemetery

Manarola
Vineyard Trail

**WALK
ENDS**

VIA **13** DEI GIOVANNI

BEST
VIEW

*Piazza
Capellini*

14

SWIMMING
& SHOWER

"MAIN STREET"

VIA

11

9

5

V. BELVEDERE

**WALK
BEGINS**

V. BALURADO

VIA BIROLLI

10

7

VIA

50 Meters
50 Yards

To
Vernazza

BOAT
DOCK

VIA DI MEZZO

VIA
BELVEDERE

*Piazza
Castello*

BREAKWATER

BOAT
DOCK

*Piazzetta
Eugenio Montale*

To
Riomaggiore

*Ligurian
Sea*

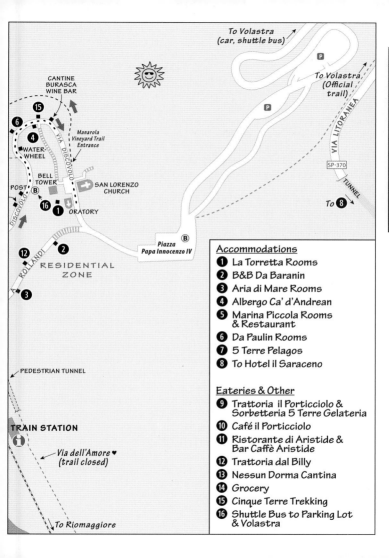

CANTINE
BURASCA
WINE BAR

To Volastra
(car, shuttle bus)

To Volastra
(Official
trail)

Manarola
Vineyard Trail
Entrance

WATER-
WHEEL

BELL
TOWER

SAN LORENZO
CHURCH

POST

ORATORY

VIA DISCOVOLO

VIA LITORANEA

SP-370

TUNNEL

To 8

Piazza
Papa Innocenzo IV

RESIDENTIAL
ZONE

ROLLANDI

PEDESTRIAN TUNNEL

TRAIN STATION

Via dell'Amore ♥
(trail closed)

To Riomaggiore

Accommodations
1. La Torretta Rooms
2. B&B Da Baranin
3. Aria di Mare Rooms
4. Albergo Ca' d'Andrean
5. Marina Piccola Rooms & Restaurant
6. Da Paulin Rooms
7. 5 Terre Pelagos
8. To Hotel il Saraceno

Eateries & Other
9. Trattoria il Porticciolo & Sorbetteria 5 Terre Gelateria
10. Café il Porticciolo
11. Ristorante di Aristide & Bar Caffè Aristide
12. Trattoria dal Billy
13. Nessun Dorma Cantina
14. Grocery
15. Cinque Terre Trekking
16. Shuttle Bus to Parking Lot & Volastra

road bends sharply right, watch (on the right) for a **waterwheel.** This recalls the origin of the town's name—local dialect for "big wheel" (one of many possible derivations). Mills like this once powered the local industry. As you continue up (all the way to the church), you'll still hear the rushing waters of Manarola's stream. Like the streams in Riomaggiore, Monterosso, and Vernazza, Manarola's rivulet was covered over after World War II. Before that time, romantic bridges arched over its ravine. You can peek below the concrete street in several places to see the stream surging below your feet.

Across the street from the waterwheel and a bit farther up, notice the **Cinque Terre Trekking** shop on your left, which outfits hikers with both information and gear (for details, see "Hikes from Manarola," later).

Around the corner is **Cantine Burasca** wine bar with fine outdoor seating (closed Wed, Via Discovolo 86, mobile 339-807-1261).

▶ *Keep climbing until you come to the square at the...*

Top of Manarola

The square is faced by a church, an oratory—now a religious and community meeting place—and a bell tower (with a WWI memorial etched in it), which served as a watchtower when pirates raided the town (the cupola was added once the attacks ceased). To the right of the oratory, a stepped lane leads to the town's sizable tourist-free residential zone.

Check out the **church.** The Parish Church of St. Lawrence (San Lorenzo) dates from "MCCCXXXVIII" (1338). Step inside to see two altarpiece paintings from the unnamed Master of the Cinque Terre, the only painter of any note from this region (left wall and above main altar). While the style is Gothic, the work dates from the time of Michelangelo, long after Florence had entered the Renaissance. Note the humble painted stone ceiling, which replaced the wooden original in the 1800s. It features Lawrence, patron saint of the Cinque Terre, with his grill, the symbol of his martyrdom (he was roasted on it).

▶ *With the bell tower on your left, head about 20 yards back down the main street below the church and find a wooden railing on the right. It marks the start of a delightful stroll around the high side of town, and back to the seafront. This is the beginning of the...*

Enjoy the views along Manarola's vineyard walk.

Manarola Vineyard Trail

Don't miss this experience. Simply follow the wooden railing, enjoying lemon groves and great views. Along the path, which is primarily flat, you'll get a close-up look at the region's famous dry-stone walls and finely crafted vineyards (with dried-heather thatches to protect the grapes from southwest winds). Smell the rosemary. Study the structure of the town, and pick out the scant remains of an old fort. Notice the S-shape of the main road—once a riverbed—that flows through town. The town's roofs are traditionally made of locally quarried slate and held down by rocks during windstorms.

Halfway along the lip of the ravine, a path marked *Panoramico Volastra (Corniglia)* leads steeply up into the vineyards (a challenging route that leads to the tiny hamlet of Volastra and then to Corniglia—described on page 26).

Stick with your level path, passing a variety of simple wooden religious scenes, the work of local resident Mario Andreoli. Before his father died, Mario promised him he'd replace the old cross on the family's vineyard. Mario has been adding figures ever since. On religious holidays, everything's lit up: the Nativity, the Last Supper, the Crucifixion, the Resurrection, and more. Some of the scenes are left up year-round.

(You can see more of his figures across the ravine, gathered together in a little open patch between buildings.) High above, notice ancient terraces that line the terrain like a topographic map.

▶ *Continue on the trail as it winds down to the cemetery. While the cemetery is closed to the public, you can stop by the gate for a peek inside.*

Cemetery

Ever since Napoleon—who was king of Italy in the early 1800s—decreed that cemeteries were health risks, Cinque Terre's burial spots have been located outside the towns. The result: The dearly departed generally get first-class sea views. Each cemetery—with evocative photos and finely carved Carrara marble memorial reliefs—is worth a look. (Manarola's is the most easily accessible.)

In cemeteries like these, the wealthy get their own piece of land (a **grave**), regular people get the equivalent of a condo (with their remains parked in a niche called a **loculus**), and the poor and forgotten end up tossed in a communal **ossuary.** Because of the tight space, spots are rented and a person's remains are allowed to stay only as long as their loved ones pay the rent. (No rent means you end up in the ossuary.) Traditionally, locals make weekly visits to loved ones here, often bringing flowers. The rolling stepladder makes access to top-floor loculi easy.

▶ *From the cemetery follow the steep and narrow stairs (through the green gate immediately below the cemetery) and walk out onto the bluff.*

Punta Bonfiglio

This point offers some of the most commanding **views** of the entire region. To find the best vantage point, walk out toward the water through a park (playground, drinking water, WC, and picnic benches).

Manarola's cemetery has a sea view…

…as do its scenic and winding trails.

An inviting and recommended bar, **Nessun Dorma,** fills a long narrow terrace with people enjoying the vista.

Your Manarola finale is the bench at the tip of the point. (It's often congested with travelers whose Instagram bucket list includes taking a photo from this point.) Pause and take in the view.

▶ *From here steps go down and the path winds scenically back to the harbor, where we started.*

EXPERIENCES IN MANAROLA

Hikes from Manarola

The coastal trail from Manarola—leading to **Corniglia** in one direction and to **Riomaggiore** in the other (the famous Via dell'Amore)—has been closed for years due to landslides. But you can still enjoy hiking from here.

One of my favorite easy hikes is to head up into the **vineyards above Manarola,** then drop down into the town cemetery, enjoying great views on the way. This route is outlined in my "Manarola Walk," earlier.

For a longer hike, consider taking the **high route to Corniglia via Volastra** (much easier if you ride the shuttle bus, rather than hike, up to Volastra). For details, see "Hiking the Cinque Terre" on page 20.

Hiking Gear and Tips: A wonderful resource for hikers, **Cinque Terre Trekking** is near the top of the main street (halfway up to the church). Christine and Nicola are generous with hiking advice, and fill their shop with all the hiking gear you may need: boots, clothes, walking sticks, maps, and more. If you're serious about hiking, stop in here to confirm your plans and to gear up (daily 11:00-13:00 & 14:00-19:00, shorter hours off-season, Via Discovolo 108, tel. 0187-920-834, www.cinqueterretrekking.com, info@cinqueterretrekking.com).

Pesto Making

Entrepreneurial Simone at the Nessun Dorma cantina (perched next to the cemetery at the most scenic edge of Manarola) leads a pesto-making workshop for up to 30 people at 10:30, followed by lunch at noon. The setting is unforgettable, making pesto in the place of its origin is exciting, and you get to eat what you make plus a *tagliere* plate of cold cuts (€50/person, includes wine, no class on Tue, reserve ahead at www.nessundormacinqueterre.com or call mobile 340-888-4133, canceled in bad weather).

Tours
Arbaspàa arranges vineyard wine tastings, cooking classes (6-person minimum), fishing trips, paragliding, rock climbing, and more (see website for options and book in advance, www.arbaspaa.com; Explora office at Via Discovolo 204, tel. 0187-920-783).

Boat Rides
To get to the dock and the boats that connect Manarola with the other Cinque Terre towns, find the steps to the left of the harbor view—they lead down to the ticket kiosk. Continue around the left side of the cliff (as you're facing the water) to catch the boats.

SLEEPING IN MANAROLA

Manarola has some of the most appealing, well-run accommodations in the region (rivaling Monterosso's). Like the others, it also has plenty of private rooms (Airbnb has consumed the market). If you need breakfast, the recommended Bar Caffè Aristide is your best choice. Otherwise grab a coffee and croissant along the main drag.

In the Residential Zone Above the Church
This area is a 10-minute steeply uphill hike from the train station—just huff up the main drag to the church. All are within a five-minute walk from there.

$$$$ La Torretta offers 14 trendy, upscale rooms (most with private deck) that cater to an elite clientele. Probably the most elegant retreat in the region, this peaceful refuge has all the comforts for those happy to pay, including a communal hot tub with a view. Guests enjoy a complementary snack and glass of prosecco on arrival, an ample breakfast buffet, daily happy hour, and stocked minibars. Each chic room is distinct (top-end family suite, book several months in advance, closed Dec-March; on request, they'll pick you up at the station tunnel in a golf cart; on Piazza della Chiesa beside the bell tower at Vico Volto 20, tel. 0187-920-327, www.torrettas.com, torretta@cdh.it, Sonia).

$$$ **B&B Da Baranin,** with eight good rooms and one apartment, is a bit too pricey but has sleek modern style and a nice breakfast terrace (family rooms, air-con, Via Aldo Rollandi 29, tel. 0187-920-595, www.baranin.com, info@baranin.com, Sara).

$$ **Aria di Mare Rooms** rents four sunny, tidy, well-equipped rooms and two apartments a few steps beyond Trattoria dal Billy at the very top of town. While it's a steep hike up (high above the tourists), this is an excellent value. Three rooms have spacious terraces, and all can enjoy the knockout views from lounge chairs in the front yard (RS%, no breakfast but tea/coffee service in room, air-con, up the stairs at Via Aldo Rollandi 149, mobile 349-058-4155, www.ariadimare.info, info@ariadimare.info, Maurizio; ask at Billy's if no one's home).

On or near the Main Street

These options line up along (or near) the main street, between the harbor and the church. While in a less atmospheric area than the ones near the church, they're closer to the station—and therefore a bit handier for those packing heavy.

$$$ **Albergo Ca' d'Andrean** is quiet, comfortable, and chic. It has 10 big, sunny, tranquil rooms with lots of tile. Public spaces artfully display family artifacts, and the cool garden oasis comes complete with lemon trees. If you don't mind stairs, consider one of their pricier top-floor rooms, with great terrace views (breakfast extra, air-con, up the hill at Via Discovolo 101, tel. 0187-920-040, www.cadandrean.it, info@cadandrean.it, Simone, Ariana, and Nicola).

$$$ **Marina Piccola,** a lesser value, offers 12 stylish rooms near the bustle of the square on the water (some with sea views). It's expensive and impersonal, but it's handy to the harbor area (air-con, Via Birolli 120, tel. 0187-920-770, www.hotelmarinapiccola.com, info@hotelmarinapiccola.com, Jessica and Micaela).

$$ **Da Paulin,** run by charming Donatella (who makes a mean *limoncello*) and Eraldo (the town's retired policeman), has three surprisingly modern, fresh, well-equipped, hotelesque rooms with a large and inviting common living room. They also rent three apartments (with fans). This fine value is at the bend in the main street, a five-minute hike above the train tracks (breakfast extra, air-con, Via Discovolo 126, mobile 334-389-4764, www.dapaulin.it, prenotazioni@dapaulin.it).

$$ **5 Terre Pelagos** has eight pastel, shabby-chic rooms in an awkward building down a side lane. Built into the side of the

mountain, the common room has a caveman ambience; some rooms come with view terraces (air-con, Via dei Mulini 26, mobile 335-122-6490, www.5terrepelagos.com, info@5terrepelagos.com, Edoardo).

High Above Manarola, in Volastra

$$ Hotel il Saraceno, with seven spacious, utilitarian rooms, is a deal for drivers. Located above Manarola in the tiny town of Volastra (chock-full of vacationing Germans and Italians in summer), it's serene, clean, and right by the shuttle bus to Manarola (free parking, air-con, tel. 0187-760-081, www.thesaraceno.com, hotel@thesaraceno.com, friendly Antonella).

EATING IN MANAROLA

Via Discovolo, the main street climbing up through town from Piazza Capellini to the church, is lined with simple places and some small grocery stores where you can browse for a picnic. This strip—and the short street between the elevated square and the harbor—also has several focaccia, pizza-by-the-slice, and fried-goodies takeaway shops that are fine for a quick lunch. **Bar Caffè Aristide** is the busiest for breakfast. And the most enticing *gelateria* in town is **Sorbetteria 5 Terre Gelateria** (a couple of doors away).

Most of the town's (touristy) restaurants are concentrated between Piazza Capellini and the harbor. The Scorza family works hard at **$$ Trattoria il Porticciolo** (Thu-Tue 12:00-21:30, closed Wed, Via Birolli 92, tel. 0187-920-083) and at their contemporary **cafè,** cheap and fast, across the way. At the harborfront, **$$$ Marina Piccola** is famous for great views, lousy service, and overcharging naive tourists.

$$$ Ristorante di Aristide, right on Piazza Capellini, is run by three generations of hardworking women and offers a trendy atmosphere and a pleasant outdoor setting, with a view of budding soccer stars rather than harborfront glitz (Fri-Wed 12:00-22:30, closed Thu, Via Discovolo 290—you run right into it from the train tunnel, tel. 0187-920-000).

$$ Bar Caffè Aristide, next door, is a busy and modern little place. They have indoor and streetside seating, a lighter menu (see daily specials on blackboard), and breakfast options (Fri-Wed 8:00-11:30 &

12:00-16:00, closed Thu, same address and phone number; charming Elena, Mamma Monica, and Nonna Grazia). Sharing a serious kitchen with Ristorante di Aristide gives this little joint an extra dose of quality.

$$$ Trattoria dal Billy, possibly the best restaurant in town, is in the residential zone high above the touristy action. Many find it's worth the climb for Edoardo and chef Enrico's homemade black pasta with seafood and squid ink, green pasta with artichokes, and homemade desserts. Their *antipasto misto di mare* comes with a dazzling array of seafood treats—each one perfectly executed. Billy's outdoor terraces offer commanding views over Manarola, while across the street an elegant, glassy dining room is carved into the rock. Either setting is perfect for a romantic candlelight meal. Reservations are a must (Fri-Wed 12:00-15:00 & 18:00-22:00, closed Thu, Via Aldo Rollandi 122, tel. 0187-920-628, www.trattoriabilly.com).

$$ Nessun Dorma Cantina is scenically perched under the cemetery and above the harbor. While they have no kitchen, Simone and his staff keep the masses happy with bruschetta, cold cuts, salads, and lots of drinks (Wed-Mon 12:00-21:00, closed Tue, Localita Punta Bonfiglio, mobile 340-888-4133). Simone runs a morning pesto-making class (described earlier, under "Experiences in Manarola").

Riomaggiore

The most substantial town of the group, Riomaggiore is a disappoint-
ment from the train station. But just walk through the tunnel next to
the tracks, and you'll discover a more real and laid-back town than its
more touristy neighbors. The main drag, while traffic-free, feels more
urban than "village," and surrounding the harbor is a fascinating tan-
gle of pastel homes leaning on each other like drunken sailors. Despite
Riomaggiore's workaday soul, the views back on its harbor from the
breakwater—especially at sunset—are some of the region's prettiest.

ORIENTATION TO RIOMAGGIORE

Tourist Information

The **info point** in the station is for train info and tickets. The adjacent striped building, with a **national park shop** and info desk, is best for visitor information (both open daily 8:00-20:00, shorter hours off-season). Amy and Francesco at Riomaggiore Reservations or Ivo and Alberto at the recommended Bar Centrale are also good sources if you're in a pinch.

Arrival in Riomaggiore

By Train: Riomaggiore's train station is separated from the town center by a bluff. To get to the center, take the pedestrian tunnel that parallels the rail tunnel. You'll exit at the bottom of Via Colombo; most recommended accommodations are a short hike up this steep main drag.

If you're staying near the top of town, you can catch the sporadic shuttle bus at the bottom of Via Colombo and ride it partway up. For a scenic route into town (for those not carrying luggage), take my "Riomaggiore Walk," later.

By Car: Day-trippers park at the two-story pay-and-display lot above town (€5/hour, €35/day). If you're staying overnight, your hotel may have parking. It is easier to park at La Spezia's train station (see the next chapter) and ride the train in.

Helpful Hints

Baggage Storage: You can check your bag at the casually run ***deposito bagagli*** office—it's behind the café/bar that's straight ahead

Workaday Riomaggiore feels lived in.　　　Here, every day is laundry day.

as you exit the station (your fee supports the sports club, daily 9:00-12:00 & 14:00-19:00—confirm times, closed in winter).

Services: There are three public pay WCs in town: at the station and at the top and bottom of Via Colombo.

Laundry: A self-service launderette is on the main street (daily in summer 8:00-20:00, shorter hours off-season, Via Colombo 107).

RIOMAGGIORE WALK

Here's an easy self-guided walk that loops up and over, taking the long and scenic way from the station into town. You'll enjoy some fine views before strolling down the main street to the harbor.

▶ *Start at the train station. (If you arrive by boat, cross beneath the tracks and take a left, then hike through the tunnel along the tracks to reach the station.)*

Climb to the Top of Town

With your back to the sea and station, look left and notice the stairs climbing up just past the station building. These lead to the easy (but closed) trail to Manarola, the **Via dell'Amore.**

Hike up the main street. Listen to the paved-over creek under your feet and at the first turn see the waterfall (and turtles in the cage). Farther along is a close-up look at dry-stone rockery work. Look down on the historic train line. Soon you'll pass the top of a concrete elevator tower (an example of local ineptitude—built but never reliably functional and now abandoned). A bit farther, you'll arrive at a fine **viewpoint,** with spectacular sea views.

▶ *When you're ready to move on, hook left around the bluff; rounding the bend, ignore the steps marked marina seacoast (which lead to the harbor) and continue another five minutes along the main (level) path toward the church. Along the way, consider a steep little side trip to the castle.*

Riomaggiore Castle

A steep stepped lane on the left leads to the castle (€2, daily 10:30-13:30). Taking this five-minute side trip, you'll find a humble art and heritage exhibit, the town's only well-preserved mural by Argentinian

To Manarola
(trail closed)

♥ Via dell'Amore ♥
(trail closed)

Cliffs

TRAIN STATION

WALK BEGINS

ABANDONED ELEVATOR

NATIONAL PARK SHOP

SAN ROCCO
CASTLE
V. PECUNIA

CITY HALL

PEDESTRIAN TUNNEL

VIA SIGNORINI

VIA SANT'ANTONIO

Piazza Vignaioli

PUNTA

Cliffs

WC (UNDER TUNNEL)

VIA SAN GIACOMO

To Manarola

To Porto Venere

Harbor

BOAT DOCK

BREAKWATER

BOAT TICKETS

Ligurian Sea

Accommodations

1. Edi's Rooms
2. Riomaggiore Reservations (Office) & Il Pescato Cucinato
3. Alla Marina Rooms; Enoteca & Ristorante Dau Cila
4. Casato Bapò
5. Il BoMa Rooms
6. La Dolce Vita Rooms

Eateries & Other

7. Rio Bistrot
8. Trattoria la Grotta
9. Bar Centrale & Gelateria
10. Primo Piatto & Vertical Lounge Bar
11. Tutti Fritti
12. Alimentari Franca
13. Bar Stazione
14. Bar & Vini A Piè de Mà
15. La Zorza Café & Bar O'Netto
16. La Conchiglia Café/Bar
17. Grocery (2)
18. Bag Storage
19. Launderette
20. Diving Center 5 Terre

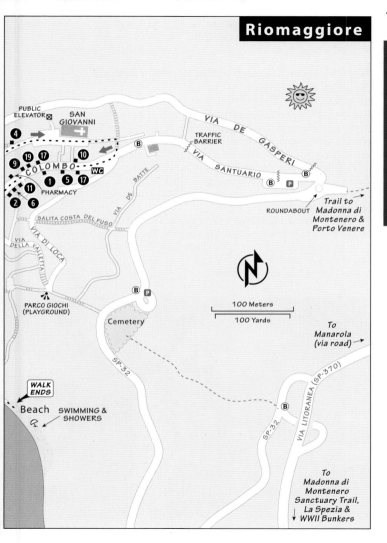

PUBLIC ELEVATOR

SAN GIOVANNI

VIA DE GASPERI

TRAFFIC BARRIER

4

VIA SANTUARIO

9 19 17

COLOMBO

10

WC

VIA DE BATTE.

11

1 5 17

PHARMACY

2 6

SALITA COSTA DEL FUSO

ROUNDABOUT

Trail to Madonna di Montenero & Porto Venere

VIA DI LOCA

VIA DELLA VALLETTA

PARCO GIOCHI (PLAYGROUND)

Cemetery

100 Meters

100 Yards

To Manarola (via road)

SP 32

WALK ENDS

Beach

SWIMMING & SHOWERS

SP 32

VIA LITORANEA (SP-370)

To Madonna di Montenero Sanctuary Trail, La Spezia & WWII Bunkers

artist Silvio Benedetto, great sea views, and the tiny church of San Rocco (built for plague victims, and therefore outside of the town walls). More of Benedetto's murals are near the City Hall.

Town Views and Church of San Giovanni Battista (St. John the Baptist)

Back down on the smooth and level lane, you'll go by the **City Hall** and several decaying **murals** (also by Silvio Benedetto), celebrating the heroic grape-pickers and fishermen of the region. These beautiful murals, with subjects modeled after real-life Riomaggiorians, glorify the nameless workers who constructed the nearly 300 million cubic feet of mortarless, dry-stone walls that run throughout the Cinque Terre. These walls give the region its characteristic *muri a secco* terracing for vineyards and olive groves. Unfortunately, the murals are not aging well.

Pause at the big **terrace** to enjoy the views of town and perhaps lots of local kids (the preschool is nearby). The major river of this region once ran through this valley, as implied by the name Riomaggiore (local dialect for "river" and "major"). As in the other Cinque Terre towns, the main street covers its *rio maggiore,* which carved the

A Silvio Benedetto mural celebrates working-class Ligurians.

canyon now filled by the town's pastel high-rises. The romantic arched bridges that once connected the two sides have been replaced by a practical modern road. Other than that, the town is beautifully preserved.

The **church,** while rebuilt in 1870, was first established in 1340. It's dedicated to St. John the Baptist, the patron saint of Genoa, the maritime republic that once dominated the region.

▶ *Continue straight past the church and along the narrow lane leading down to the town's main street...*

Via Colombo

Heading down the hill on Via Colombo, you'll pass several handy fast-food joints. (A hot political issue lately: too many fast-food joints and no place to sit.) Farther along, the big covered terrace on the right belongs to the recommended **Bar Centrale,** a popular hangout for international visitors day or night.

As you round the bend to the left, notice the old-timey pharmacy just above (on the right, with a good bakery underneath). On your left, at #199, peek into the **Il Pescato Cucinato** shop, where Laura fries up her husband Edoardo's fresh catch; grab a paper cone of deep-fried seafood as a snack. Where the road bends sharply right, notice the bench on your left (just before La Zorza Café)—the hangout for the town's old-timers, who keep a running commentary on the steady flow of people. Straight ahead, you can already see where this street will dead-end. The last shop on the left, **Alimentari Franca** (at #251), is a well-stocked grocery where you can gather the makings for a perfect picnic out on the harbor.

Where Via Colombo dead-ends, look right to see the tunnel leading back to the station. Look left to see two sets of stairs. Climb the "up" stairs to a parklike **square** (Piazza Vignaioli) built over the train tracks, which provides the children of the town a bit of level land on which to kick their soccer balls and to learn to ride a bike. The murals above, marking the town's middle school, celebrate the great-grandparents of these very children—the salt-of-the-earth locals who earned a humble living before the age of tourism. Riomaggiorians are proud that they are the only Cinque Terre town with their own middle school—in the other towns, kids are sent away to school much earlier.

▶ *Take the "down" stairs to the...*

Riomaggiore's beach scene is busy by day... ...and romantic by night.

Harbor

This most picturesque corner of Riomaggiore features a tight cluster of buildings huddling nervously around a tiny square and harbor. Because Riomaggiore lacks the naturally protected harbor of
Vernazza, when bad weather is expected, fishermen pull their boats
up to the safety of the little square. This is quite an operation, so it's a
team effort—the signal goes out, and anyone with a boat of their own
helps move the whole fleet. Sometimes the fishermen are busy beach-
ing their boats even on a bright, sunny day—an indication that they
know something you don't.

A couple of recommended restaurants—with high prices and
memorable seating—look down over the action. Head past them and
up the walkway along the left side of the harbor, and enjoy the **views**
back at the town's colorful pastel buildings, with the craggy coast-
line of the Cinque Terre just beyond. The best views are from up top,
at the edge of the bluff. Below you, the breakwater (made of reject
marble blocks from the famous nearby quarries of Carrara) curves
out to sea, providing a bit of protection for the harbor. These rocks
are popular with sunbathers by day and romantics and photogra-
phers at sunset.

For a peek at Riomaggiore's **beach,** continue around the bluff on
this trail toward Punta di Montenero, the cape that defines the southern end of the Cinque Terre. As you walk, you'll pass the rugged boat
landing and eventually run into Riomaggiore's uncomfortably rocky
but still inviting beach (*spiaggia*). Ponder how Europeans manage to
look relaxed when lounging on football-sized "pebbles."

EXPERIENCES IN RIOMAGGIORE

Hikes from Riomaggiore

For an **easy walk** along the lip of the one-time river ravine, take **Via di Loca,** which veers off the main drag at the top of town (directly across from the stairs at the upper end of Via Colombo). This leads in just a few minutes to the town playground (*parco giochi*), benches, neighborhood pea patches, and pleasant views over town (especially at sunset). There's also a steep staircase from here up to the town cemetery; from there, an even steeper trail runs all the way up to the town's sanctuary (or see the easier alternative—described next).

For a **scenic one-hour trail** that rises from Riomaggiore to the 14th-century **Madonna di Montenero sanctuary,** high above the town, take the main road inland until you see signs at the roundabout at the top of town; or ride the shuttle bus 12 minutes from the town center to the sanctuary trail, then walk uphill another 20 minutes (great picnic spot up top).

Beach

Riomaggiore's rugged and tiny "beach" is rocky, but it's clean and peaceful. It's just around the bluff from the harbor, past the boat

landing—to find it, see the end of my self-guided walk, earlier. There's a shower here in the summer, and another closer to town by the boat landing—where many enjoy sunning on and jumping from the rocks.

Kayaks and Water Sports

Diving Center 5 Terre rents kayaks as well as snorkeling and scuba equipment; they also lead guided dives of the protected marine waters nearby (daily May-Sept 9:00-18:00, open only in good weather, likely weekends only in shoulder season, office down the stairs and under the tracks on Via San Giacomo, tel. 0187-920-011, www.5terrediving.it).

NIGHTLIFE IN RIOMAGGIORE

With a youthful spirit and lively evening bustle, Riomaggiore has an enjoyable night scene. Stroll the main drag, scope out these listings (serving €6-8 cocktails), and find the one that appeals. Several of these places have full menus if you want to eat.

Bar Centrale, run by sociable Ivo, Alberto, and the gang, offers "nightlife" any time of day—it's a magnet for tourists. Ivo, who lived in

Riomaggiore's breakwater is the perfect spot to watch the sun go down and the lights come up.

the Bay Area, fills his bar with San Franciscan rock and a fun-loving vibe; it feels a little like the village's living room (great mojitos, daily 7:30-late, Via Colombo 144).

Bar & Vini A Piè de Mà, above the train station at the now closed Via dell'Amore trailhead, has piles of charm, frequent music, and stays open until midnight from June through September.

More Bars and Cafés: Near the bottom of Via Colombo, facing each other, are the noisy **La Zorza Café** (appealing to international tourists with thumping music and freestyle bartender) and the classier **Bar O'Netto** (geared more for young locals, with a mellower vibe and nice outdoor seating). Higher up on Via Colombo (at #76), **Vertical Lounge Bar** has a lively and loose ambience, light food (a good *aperitivo* buffet at happy-hour time), and a fine people-watching perch near the top of the promenade zone. And at sunset, you can't beat **La Conchiglia**—the simple café/bar on the bluff overlooking the harbor—a perfect location for watching the sun disappear into the Ligurian Sea and the lights of Monterosso twinkling on the horizon.

SLEEPING IN RIOMAGGIORE

Riomaggiore has few hotels worth your time; I recommend staying in one of the town's many private rooms for rent. Very few private rooms include breakfast.

Room-Booking Services

A couple of room-booking agencies—with relatively predictable office hours, English-speaking staff, and email addresses—are next to each other on Via Colombo. Each manages a corral of local rooms for rent; the quality and specific amenities can vary wildly, so get a complete picture of the room before you commit. It's smart to settle up the day before you leave in case they're closed when you need to depart. Expect lots of stairs—ask how many when you book.

$$ Edi's Rooms manages four double rooms and eight apartments. You pay extra for views (most rooms with air-con, office open daily in summer 9:00-13:00 & 14:00-19:30, closed Nov-Feb, reception at Via Colombo 111, tel. 0187-920-325, www.appartamenticinqueterre.net, edi-vesigna@iol.it).

$ Riomaggiore Reservations, run with care by American expat Amy and her Italian husband, Francesco, offers six rooms and four apartments (RS%, cash only, reception open daily 9:00-13:00 & 14:00-17:00 in season, air-con, Via Colombo 181, tel. 0187-760-575, www. riomaggiorereservations.com, info@riomaggiorereservations.com). They're a great resource for info on hiking and other activities.

Rooms for Rent (*Affittacamere*)

Another option is to book directly with someone who rents just a few rooms of their own.

$$ Alla Marina is Riomaggiore's best value, with five rooms—most with sea views—at the top of one of the tall, skinny buildings that rise up from the harbor. Friendly brothers Sandro and Andrea take pride in running a tight ship. They also rent four apartments and several rooms in other parts of town (RS%—free breakfast at nearby café, air-con, pay parking, office open 9:00-18:00, Via San Giacomo 61—ask about the easier back-door entrance, mobile 328-013-4077, www. allamarina.com, info@allamarina.com).

$$ Casato Bapò has three airy, spacious rooms with unobstructed views at the top of town near the Church of San Giovanni. They're on the fourth floor, but accessible via the public elevator nearby (Via Pecunia 116, mobile 340-705-6723, www.casatobapo.com, casatobapo@gmail.com, Sabrina).

$$ Il BoMa—named for the owners, American Maddy and her Italian husband, Bombetta—has three old-fashioned rooms along the main drag (one cheaper room with private bath down the hall, air-con, up three flights at Via Colombo 99, tel. 0187-920-395, mobile 320-0748826, www.ilboma.itcom, info@ilboma.it). They also rent two nearby apartments.

$$ La Dolce Vita offers six modern, good-value rooms on the main drag, plus two apartments elsewhere in town (some with air-con, no breakfast, open daily 9:30-19:30—if they're closed, they're full; Via Colombo 167, tel. 0187-920-935, agonatal@libero.it, helpful Giacomo and Simone).

EATING IN RIOMAGGIORE

For more options, see "Nightlife in Riomaggiore," earlier.

On the Harbor

Harborfront dining comes with slightly higher prices, a dressy ambience, and glorious views. These two eateries share the same owner; the first one's menu is more traditionally Italian, while the second is a bit more modern.

$$$$ Enoteca & Ristorante Dau Cila (pronounced "dow CHEE-lah") is decked out like a black-and-white movie set in an old boat shed with extra tables outside on a rustic deck over dinghies. Try their antipasto specialty of several seafood appetizers (dinner only) and listen to the waves lapping at the harbor below (cheaper lunch menu with salads and *bruschette,* daily 12:00-24:00, Via San Giacomo 65, tel. 0187-760-032, Niccolo).

$$$$ Rio Bistrot, small and intimate at the top of the harbor, tries to jazz up its Ligurian cuisine with international influences. You can order à la carte from the short but well-designed menu, or try their €39 tasting menu (simpler and cheaper lunch menu, daily 12:00-16:00 & 18:00-22:00, Via San Giacomo 46, tel. 0187-920-616, Manuel).

On the Main Street, Via Colombo

$$ Trattoria la Grotta, right in the town center (with no view), has a passion for anchovies and mussels. You'll enjoy reliably good food surrounded by historical photos and wonderful stonework in a dramatic, dressy, cave-like setting (daily 12:00-14:30 & 17:30-22:30, closed Wed in winter, Via Colombo 247, tel. 0187-920-187).

$$ Bar Centrale is a casual, family-friendly place for hamburgers, salads, and pesto. They also have a *gelateria* on site (long hours daily, see listing earlier, under "Nightlife in Riomaggiore").

Light Meals: Various handy takeaway eateries along the main drag offer good lunches or snacks. **$ Primo Piatto,** at the top of town, offers takeaway handmade pastas and sauces, cooked to order on the spot (Wed-Mon 10:30-19:30 or later, closed Tue, Via Colombo 72, Roberta). For deep-fried seafood in a paper cone, **$ Il Pescato Cucinato** is where Edoardo fishes and his wife, Laura, fries (chalkboard out front explains what's fresh, daily 11:20-20:30, near the bottom of Via Colombo at #199). A few doors away, **$ Tutti Fritti** serves

Enjoy a coffee from your perch above the sea near the station.

only fried nibbles, including fish (daily 10:00-21:00, Via Colombo 161, Andrea and Isabella).

Picnics: Groceries and delis lining Via Colombo sell food to-go for a picnic at the harbor or beach. **Co-op** grocery stores (several on the main drag) have the best prices. For a more appetizing selection and good service, head to **Alimentari Franca,** on the main street by the train-station tunnel (daily 8:00-20:00, Via Colombo 251).

Breakfast: Most of my recommended accommodations don't serve breakfast—or simply leave a coffee kettle and basic continental breakfast fixings in your room. For eggs or a good croissant-and-espresso fix, drop by **Bar Centrale** (listed earlier); or **Bar Stazione,** at the train station.

Near the Train Station

$$ Bar & Vini A Piè de Mà, at the trailhead on the Manarola end of town, is good for a scenic light bite or quiet drink at night. The bar, with great outdoor seating, is self-service: Head into the bar to place your order, then bring it out to your preferred perch (daily 10:00-20:00, June-Sept until 24:00, closed Mon-Tue off-season, tel. 0187-921-037).

Near the Cinque Terre

The Cinque Terre is tops, but there's much more to the Italian Riviera. To the north of the Cinque Terre is a trio of beach towns: Levanto, the northern gateway to the Cinque Terre; Sestri Levante, stunningly situated on a narrow peninsula flanked by two beaches; and Santa Margherita Ligure, a thriving city with an active waterfront and easy connections to yacht-happy Portofino. At the south end of the Cinque Terre is the pretty resort of Porto Venere and the region's gritty transit hub, La Spezia.

The best of these towns—the high-end yin to the Cinque Terre's ramshackle yang—can be user-friendly home bases for day trips along the Riviera coast. But they are also worth visiting in their own right.

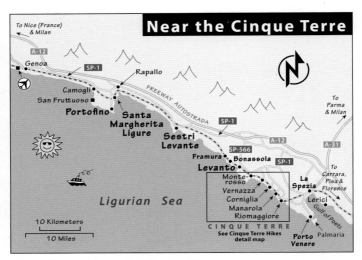

Home Bases Near the Cinque Terre

Levanto, Sestri Levante, and Santa Margherita Ligure are practical home bases for drivers wanting to park at their hotel and side-trip to the Cinque Terre by train, or for those who want modern hotels with predictable resort amenities. (They're also worth a look if the Cinque Terre is booked up.)

Levanto—just minutes north of Monterosso by train—is the handiest. Sestri Levante is a bit farther away with a little less train service. Santa Margherita Ligure is the most distant and often requires a transfer to the Cinque Terre, but compensates by being the most appealing—and it has easy access to posh Portofino. Porto Venere is better as a day trip, and La Spezia is more functional than appealing, although either can serve in a pinch.

If you home-base near the Cinque Terre, keep in mind that you'll be competing with other day-trippers for space on prime midday trains to and from the Cinque Terre. Turn this problem into an advantage: Enjoy your home-base town during the day, then head into the Cinque Terre in the late afternoon for untrampled charm, a romantic dinner, and a late train back.

North of the Cinque Terre

When most people imagine the "Italian Riviera," they're thinking of the shimmering resort towns north of the Cinque Terre. Stately Old World hotels loom over crowded pebble beaches with rentable umbrellas. Fastidiously landscaped parks and promenades are jammed with more Italian visitors than American tourists. These towns are perfect for day-tripping—or even an overnight.

Levanto

Graced with a long, sandy beach, Levanto (LEH-vahn-toh) is packed in summer and popular with families and surfers. The rest of the year, it's just a small, sleepy town. Although not as charming as the Cinque Terre, it enjoys fewer crowds, more varied hotel and dining options, and quick connections to the Cinque Terre (4 minutes to Monterosso by train, continuing to the rest of the Cinque Terre villages on the same line).

This beach town isn't the "real" Cinque Terre, but it can be a friendly home base (with a high number of family rooms and large, affordable apartments with kitchenettes.) From Levanto, you can hop a train or boat to the Cinque Terre towns and beyond; take the no-wimps-allowed hike to Monterosso (3.5 hours); or bike or stroll on a delightful, level path to the nearby, uncrowded beach village of Bonassola.

ORIENTATION TO LEVANTO

Levanto (pop. 5,400) is dominated by an uninspiring new town, a regular grid street plan of five-story apartment buildings that stretches from the train station down to the broad, curving beach. The sleepy, twisty old town—bisected by a modern street—is tucked up against the adjacent hill.

Tourist Information

A Cinque Terre National Park info center is at the train station. The

Levanto

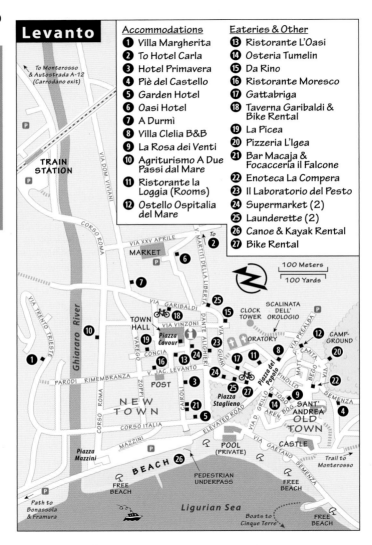

Accommodations

1. Villa Margherita
2. To Hotel Carla
3. Hotel Primavera
4. Piè del Castello
5. Garden Hotel
6. Oasi Hotel
7. A Durmì
8. Villa Clelia B&B
9. La Rosa dei Venti
10. Agriturismo A Due Passi dal Mare
11. Ristorante la Loggia (Rooms)
12. Ostello Ospitalia del Mare

Eateries & Other

13. Ristorante L'Oasi
14. Osteria Tumelin
15. Da Rino
16. Ristorante Moresco
17. Gattabriga
18. Taverna Garibaldi & Bike Rental
19. La Picea
20. Pizzeria L'Igea
21. Bar Macaja & Focacceria il Falcone
22. Enoteca La Compera
23. Il Laboratorio del Pesto
24. Supermarket (2)
25. Launderette (2)
26. Canoe & Kayak Rental
27. Bike Rental

helpful TI is on Piazza Cavour (daily 9:00-13:00 & 15:00-18:00 except closed Sun afternoon, shorter hours off-season, tel. 0187-808-125, www.visitlevanto.it).

Arrival in Levanto

By Train: From the train station (no baggage storage), head through the parking lot and down the stairs, turn right, and cross the bridge onto Corso Roma—the main drag. The beach is straight ahead, and most of my recommended hotels, restaurants, and the TI are in the grid of streets to your left. You can walk from the station to most of my recommended places in about 10 minutes.

By Car: If your hotel doesn't offer parking—or if you're not sleeping here—you have a couple of good alternatives. The lots surrounding the **train station** are affordable and handy for hopping a train to the Cinque Terre towns. If you're heading for the beach, the parking lot there is handy but more expensive.

Helpful Hints

Markets: Levanto's modern covered *mercato,* which sells produce and fish, is on Via XXV Aprile, between the train station and the beach (daily 7:30-13:00). On Wednesday morning, an **open-air market** with clothes, shoes, and housewares fills the street in front of the *mercato.*

Laundry: A **self-service launderette** stuffed with snack-and-drink vending machines is at Piazza Staglieno 38, facing an inviting park (daily 24 hours, mobile 338-701-6341). Another self-service place, **Speedy Wash,** is at Via Garibaldi 32 (daily 8:00-22:00, mobile 338-701-6341).

Bike Rental: Relatively flat Levanto, with light traffic, is a great bike town—and the ride to nearby Bonassola and Framura is easy and delightful. Try **Cicli Raso** (€10-20/day depending on bike, daily 9:30-12:30 & 15:30-19:00, closed Sun Nov-April, Via Garibaldi 63, tel. 0187-802-511) or the **Sensafreni Bike Shop,** convenient to the beach boardwalk, with well-maintained bikes (€5/hour, €8/half-day, €15/day, more for ebikes, daily 9:00-13:00 & 16:00-19:30, Piazza del Popolo 1, tel. 0187-807-128).

Sports Rentals: Right on the beach, **Rosa dei Venti** rents kayaks, canoes, surfboards, and windsurfing equipment (mobile 329-451-1981, www.levantorosadeiventi.it, Marco).

Levanto's harbor is bordered by an elevated promenade.

Electric Bike Tours: Ebikein offers a variety of guided tours on electric bikes—giving you a helpful boost on the hills. Options include a four-hour loop around the Bay of Levanto (€58) and a four-hour pedal up to some of the sanctuaries above the Cinque Terre towns (€69, www.ebikein.com, mobile 334-190-0496).

Boat Tours: Sea Breeze operates out of Monterosso but will pick you up in Levanto for full-day or *aperitivo* sunset tours. See their listing on page 43.

SIGHTS IN LEVANTO

Beach

Levanto's beach hides below a parking lot and promenade that's elevated above the sand—look for underpasses or stairs along its length. There are pretty boardwalks up on the elevated promenade and down along the beachfront. As you face the harbor, the boat dock is to your far left, and the diving center is to your far right.

In summer, three parts of the beach are free: both sides of the boat dock, and near Piazza Mazzini. The rest of the beach is broken up into private sections that you pay to enter. You can always stroll along the beach, even through the private sections—just don't sit down. Off-season, roughly October through May, the entire beach is free, and you can lay your towel anywhere you like. Ask your hotel for towels; most have beach towels to loan or rent.

Old Town

The old town clusters around Piazza del Popolo. Until a few decades ago, the town's open-air market was held at the 13th-century loggia (covered set of archways) in the square. The original medieval town spreads from Via Guani to the oratory of San Giacomo and the old clock tower, and from the loggia to the Church of Sant'Andrea (c. 1212). Levanto was once an important harbor of the Republic of Genoa; from here, shipments of olive oil, wine, and the coveted red marble *rosso levanto* set sail.

▲Hike to Monterosso

This strenuous 3.5-hour hike is described in more detail on page 28.

To begin in Levanto, start on Piazza del Popolo, and head uphill to the striped Church of Sant'Andrea. From the church courtyard, follow the sign to the *castello* (a private residence), go under the stone arch, and continue uphill. From here, take trail SVA (following signs toward Punta Mesco, the rugged tip of the peninsula), then drop steeply down into Monterosso. (If you have knee issues, consider starting in Monterosso instead.)

▲Hike or Bike to Bonassola (and Framura)

Tucked just off the main train line on a cove north of Levanto, the small beach resort of Bonassola (boh-nah-SOH-lah, pop. 950) is a peaceful little eddy. As far as Riviera beach resorts go, this is a jewel. With a low-key vibe, a tidy grid street plan that feels almost French, and a picturesque dark-sand beach hemmed in by jagged bluffs, Bonassola is a fine alternative to the region's other beaches. And the next best thing to a beach day in Bonassola is getting there: A level, easy, rails-to-trails path cuts through the mountain from Levanto—enjoyable by foot, but even better by bike.

Levanto to Bonassola: Local **trains** run between Levanto and Bonassola (hourly, 3 minutes, confirm your train will stop in Bonassola). But I'd rather take the **promenade.** At the northern end of Levanto's beachfront road/parking lot, you'll find a level, roughly 1.5-mile path neatly divided into bike and pedestrian lanes. Most of the route is through well-lit former train tunnels, with brief breaks overlooking the sea (and hikes down to secluded beaches). The walk takes about 30 minutes, with long stretches through cool tunnels; by bike, it's less than 10 minutes.

Bonassola's seaside promenade

Framura's rocky harbor

Bonassola's beach is encircled by rocky bluffs.

Visiting Bonassola: The town itself—with manicured promenades and piazzas—is worth exploring. **$$ Caffè delle Rose,** facing the town's elevated road (at Via Fratelli Rezzano 22), has good gelato, food, and drinks. Several *foccacerie* and other eateries cluster at the far end of town. The **beach** is separated from the town center by the elevated road (shared by bicyclists, walkers, and a parking lot). The inviting beach has mostly private sections, with a few free public areas.

For a scenic **walk/hike,** head to the far (north) end of the beach, where a promenade snakes along the base of the cliff (with rocky perches for sunbathing and swimming). For higher views, find the stairs near the flagpole, and follow the steps up on the right side of the yellow church. Popping out at the top, turn left along the scenic, private road as it curls around the top of the bay, with great views back on the town and beach; the path ends at the blocky little Madonnina della Punta chapel.

Bonassola to Framura (best for bicyclists): From Bonassola, the promenade continues another 1.5 miles to the town of Framura—a settlement made up of five medieval hamlets that rise up from the seafront to the hilltop (pop. 750). Because this part of the route is almost entirely through tunnels, it's boring for walkers—but quick for bikers.

The trail ends overlooking Framura's rocky little harbor and near its train station (there's no direct access to the station—don't count on taking your bike back on the train).

Visiting Framura: Park your bike at the trailhead and hike down to the harbor, cross under the train tracks, and emerge near the station and the start of the scenic Via del Mare path (basic café at trailhead). This easy promenade takes you north along a cliff face in 10 minutes to two small, pristine gravel beaches that are free and uncrowded.

SLEEPING IN LEVANTO

$$$ Villa Margherita is across the river and a bit uphill (about a 10-minute walk from the town center or train station), but the shaded view gardens, 11 colorfully tiled rooms, and tranquility are worth the walk (family rooms, air-con, elevator one flight up from street level, free parking, Via Trento e Trieste 31, tel. 0187-807-212, mobile 328-842-6934, www.villamargherita.net, info@villamargherita.net, Paola).

$$$ Hotel Carla sits in a humdrum residential zone, about 10 minutes from the beach and the station. Its 30 rooms come with contemporary style—most have balconies, and all are decorated in soothing, neutral colors (RS%, family rooms, air-con, elevator, free loaner bikes, Via Martiri della Libertà 28, tel. 0187-808-275, www.carlahotel.com, info@carlahotel.com).

$$$ Hotel Primavera is homey and family-run, with 17 colorful rooms—10 with balconies (but no views)—just a block from the beach (family rooms, request a quiet room off the street, includes hearty breakfast buffet, air-con, pay private parking, free loaner bikes, Via Cairoli 5, tel. 0187-808-023, www.primaverahotel.com, info@primaverahotel.com; friendly Carlo, cheerful Daniela, and daughters Giuditta and Gloria).

$$$ Piè del Castello is right on the Levanto-Monterosso trail. Andrea and his wife rent three double rooms, each with a patio and access to a sprawling garden with views of the ancient city wall and the Church of Sant'Andrea. Hikers will appreciate Andrea's knowledge of area trails (air-con, fridge, free parking, Via Guido Semenza 2, tel. 366-1467-7886, www.piedelcastello.com, info@piedelcastello.com).

$$$ Garden Hotel offers 17 functional, businesslike, modern rooms (all with balconies but no views) on the first floor of an apartment building. While it's a lesser value, you're paying for proximity to the beach—it's just across the street (closed Nov-mid-March, air-con, elevator, free parking off-site, loaner bikes, Corso Italia 6, tel. 0187-808-173, www.nuovogarden.com, info@nuovogarden.com, Davide and Damiano).

$$ Oasi Hotel, well-run by Silvia, has 14 rooms in a cozy small hotel behind the market hall. Some rooms have balconies, others have direct access to the garden, and a few have neither but are larger—request your choice when you reserve (RS%, air-con, elevator, parking extra, Via Ferraro, tel. 0187-807-356, www.oasihotel.eu, info@oasishotel.eu, Saverio).

$$ A Durmì is a happy little guesthouse owned by lovely Graziella, Gianni, and their two daughters, Elisa and Chiara. Their sunny patios, green leafy gardens, six immaculate beach bungalow-type rooms, and five sunlit apartments make this a welcoming place to stay (breakfast extra, family rooms, air-con, bar, pay parking, Via D. Viviani 12, tel. 0187-800-823, mobile 349-105-6016, www.adurmi.it, info@adurmi.it).

$$ Villa Clelia B&B offers five basic rooms with minifridges and terraces. The rooms surround a garden courtyard just a short walk up from the sea (minimal in-room breakfast, air-con, free parking; with the old town's loggia on your left, it's straight ahead at Piazza da Passano 1; tel. 0187-808-195, mobile 329-379-4859, www.villaclelia.it, info@villaclelia.it). Their apartments in the center economically sleep up to five.

$$ La Rosa dei Venti is an *affittacamere* just a couple of blocks from the beach, in the old town. Enthusiastic Rosanna and her son Marco rent five old-fashioned, overpriced rooms with dark hardwood floors, comfy rugs, and glittery seashore decor (air-con, pay parking, from Piazza del Popolo take the lane next to Osteria Tumelin to Via della Compera, tel. 0187-808-165, mobile 328-742-8268, www.larosadeiventilevanto.com, info@larosadeiventilevanto.com).

$ Agriturismo A Due Passi dal Mare is an in-town oasis, just a five-minute walk from the beach or the train station. Friendly Francesca and husband Maurizio rent four crisp, quiet rooms—with sizable bathrooms—in the 1920s home built by her grandfather; their back garden is open to guests (free on-site parking, closed Jan-Feb, right on the main drag at Corso Roma 37, tel. 0187-809-177, mobile 338-960-1537, www.a2passidalmare.com, info@a2passidalmare.com).

$ Ristorante la Loggia has eight cozy, older, and cheap rooms, perched above the old loggia on Piazza del Popolo (request balcony, quieter rooms in back, two basic side-by-side apartments great for families of 4-8, lots of stairs, air-con, free parking, reception open 9:00-23:00, Piazza del Popolo 7, tel. 0187-808-107, mobile 335-641-7701, www.loggialevanto.com, laloggialaloggia@gmail.com, Alessandro). They also have a recommended restaurant.

Hostel: ¢ Ostello Ospitalia del Mare, a budget gem, is run by the city tourist association. It has 70 basic beds, airy rooms, an elevator, and a terrace in a well-renovated medieval palazzo a few steps from the old town (all ages, dorms with private bath, private rooms, includes breakfast, self-service laundry, no curfew or lockout; office open daily April-Oct 8:00-12:30 & 16:00-19:30, until 23:00 weekend nights; may close Nov-March, Via San Nicolò 1, tel. 0187-802-562, www.ospitialevanto.com, info@ospitialevanto.com).

EATING IN LEVANTO

$$$$ Ristorante L'Oasi—spacious, bright, and with a garden feel— is the place for quality fish and seafood in Levanto. Family run, with Claudio in the kitchen and Lella supervising the dining room, this is a polished setting for enjoying fresh tuna tartare, marinated anchovies, and grilled swordfish (daily 12:30-14:30 & 19:00-22:30, closed Wed Sept-June, Piazza Cavour, tel. 0187-800-856).

$$$ Osteria Tumelin has a dressy ambience in its elegant dining room, a casual covered terrace out front, and a wide selection of fresh seafood. Reservations are smart on weekends or to dine outside. Check out the aquarium containing giant lobster and moray eels in the first dining room on the right (daily 12:00-14:30 & 19:00-22:30, closed Thu Oct-May, Via D. Grillo 32, across the square from the loggia, tel. 0187-808-379, www.tumelin.it).

$$ Da Rino, a small trattoria on a quiet pedestrian lane, dishes up reasonably priced seafood, meat, and homemade Ligurian specialties. Consider the grilled *totani* (squid), *pansotti con salsa di noci* (ravioli with walnut sauce), and *trofie al pesto* (pasta with pesto sauce). Dine indoors or out (Wed-Mon 19:00-22:00, closed Tue, Via Garibaldi 10, tel. 0187-813-475).

$$ Ristorante la Loggia has been dishing up classic Ligurian cuisine for more than 50 years. Choose between the homey, wood-paneled dining room with nooks and crannies or the little terrace overlooking the square (daily 12:30-14:00 & 19:00-22:00, closed Nov-Feb, Piazza del Popolo 7, tel. 0187-808-107). They also rent rooms (see previous page).

$$$ Ristorante Moresco serves large portions of pasta and sea-food at reasonable prices in a vaulted, candlelit room decorated with Moorish-style frescoes (daily 12:00-14:00 & 19:00-21:00, reserva-tions appreciated, Via Jacopo 24, tel. 0187-807-253, busy Roberto and Francesca).

$$ Gattabriga hides out on a back lane behind Piazza del Popolo with a contemporary look; an updated and well-priced menu of pastas, seafood, and meats; and friendly service (Tue-Sun 19:00-21:30, closed Mon, Via Guani 47, tel. 366-527-3582).

$$ Taverna Garibaldi, a comfy good-value place on the town's most characteristic street, serves focaccia with various toppings, made-to-order *farinata* (savory chickpea crêpe), salads, and more than 30 types of pizza (Fri-Wed 19:00-22:00, closed Thu, Via Garibaldi 57, tel. 0187-808-098).

$$ La Picea offers wood-fired pizzas and a large selection of beers to-go, or you can dine at one of their few small tables (Tue-Sun 12:00-14:00 & 19:00-24:00 or until they use up their pizza dough, closed Mon, just off Piazza Cavour at Via della Concia 18, tel. 0187-802-063).

$$ Pizzeria L'Igea is tucked inside the Campeggio Acquadolce campground, 50 yards past the hostel. It's a favorite among locals who know you don't have to be a camper to enjoy freshly made, budget-conscious pizza and pasta in their bright dining hall. Their specialty is *gattafin*—deep-fried herb-stuffed ravioli. Come early or be prepared to wait, even for takeout (daily 12:00-14:30 & 18:45-22:30, Via Guido Semenza 5, tel. 0187-807-293).

$-$$ Bar Macaja, decorated in shabby chic beach-style, is a tiny place with a big happy vibe. Stop in for a continental breakfast, espres-so or a drink, *panini,* and local seafood—including anchovies prepared six ways (Fri-Wed 7:00-23:00, closed Thu, just up from the beach at Via Cairoli 25, mobile 349-844-8424).

$ Enoteca La Compera offers a quiet respite on a hidden courtyard across the way from the campground. It's casual and friendly, serving a wide variety of *panini* that you can buy to-go, as well as plenty of wine, including affordable tastings, called *degustazione* (Tue-Sun 10:00-20:00, closed Mon, follow the red-brick road—under the stone arch—to Piazza della Compera 3, mobile 334-712-8517).

Picnics and Bites on the Go: *Focaccerie, rosticcerie,* and delis with takeout pasta abound on Via Dante Alighieri. **$ Focacceria il Falcone** has a great selection of focaccia with different toppings (daily 9:30-22:00, shorter hours off-season, Via Cairoli 19, tel. 0187-807-370). For more picnic options, try the *mercato* (see "Helpful Hints," earlier). It's fun to grab a crusty loaf of bread, then pair it with a pot of freshly made Genovese pesto and other gifty edibles from **$ Il Laboratorio del Pesto** (daily, Via Dante 14).

There are two **Crai supermarkets** (daily 8:00-20:00 except closed for lunch on Sun): One is just off Piazza Cavour at Via del Municipio 5; the other is nearby on Piazza Staglieno. For a shaded setting, lay out your spread on a bench in the grassy park at this piazza. Another fine picnic spot is Piazza Cristoforo Colombo, located east of the swimming pool, with benches and sea views.

LEVANTO CONNECTIONS

To get to the Cinque Terre from Levanto, you can take the **train** (3-4/ hour, 4 minutes to Monterosso). A slower, more scenic option is the **boat,** which stops at every Cinque Terre town (except Corniglia) before heading to Porto Venere (3/day in high season, price depends on distance traveled—or get a €35 all-day hop-on, hop-off ticket; only one return boat daily from Porto Venere—departs at about 16:30; get latest boat schedule and price sheet at TI or boat dock or check website, tel. 0187-732-987, www.navigazionegolfodeipoeti.it).

Sestri Levante

Sestri Levante (SEH-stree leh-VAHN-teh) is squeezed as skinny as a hot dog between its two beaches. The pedestrian-friendly Via XXV Aprile, which runs down the middle of the peninsula, is lined with shops that sell takeout pizza, pastries, and beach paraphernalia.

Hans Christian Andersen enjoyed his visit here in the mid-1800s, writing, "What a fabulous evening I spent in Sestri Levante!" One of the bays—Baia delle Favole—is named in his honor (*favole* means "fairy tale"). The small mermaid curled on the edge of the fountain behind the TI is another nod to the beloved Danish storyteller.

ORIENTATION TO SESTRI LEVANTE

Sestri Levante (pop. 18,000) is dominated by its big, dull modern town in front of the train station. But don't be discouraged—the old-town peninsula, a 10-minute walk away, has charm to spare.

Tourist Information: It's at Corso Colombo 50, on the ground floor of Palazzo Fascie, the town's cultural center (daily 9:00-13:00 & 14:00-17:00, shorter hours off-season, tel. 0185-478-530, www.sestri-levante.net). They can tell you about the summer bike-sharing program (€8/5 hours) and direct you to the trail (south of town) for a 1.5-hour hike (each way) to the scenic Punta Manara promontory.

Arrival in Sestri Levante: From the train station (no baggage storage), head straight out and across the piazza to go down the arcaded Via Roma. (If you need picnic supplies, you'll pass a Carrefour Express.) To reach the enjoyable pedestrian zone, the old-town peninsula, and beaches, follow the "Stroll the Town" advice on page 133.

Market Day: It's on Saturday at Piazza Aldo Moro (8:00-13:00).

Laundry: A self-service launderette is in the urban zone southeast of the train station (daily 8:30-20:30, Via Costantino Raffo 8, mobile 389-101-1454).

Sestri Levante

To Rapallo & Santa Margherita Ligure

To Santa Margherita Ligure

LUNGO. G. DESCALZO

TRAIN STATION

To Santa Margherita Ligure & Portofino

To Cinque Terre

Baia delle Favole

2

3

VIA OLIVE

Piazza Caduti

VIALE MAZZINI

V. ROMA

12

V. ERALDO

To Levanto & Cinque Terre

Piazza Italia

VIA NAZIONALE

To

Giardini Ventre

VIA XX SETT.

C. COLOMBO

Piazza Sant' Antonio

VIA

To A-12 Freeway

Piazza Repubblica

FASCIE

4

BOAT DOCK

Beaches

V. V. VENETO

VIALE V. VENETO

V. TERESA

V. DANTE

VIA RIMEMBRANZA

V. APRILE

6

Piazza Aldo Moro

PROMENADE & BIKE PATH →

11

VIA PILADE QUEIROLO

8

Piazza Matteotti

VICO CORO

VIA POZZETTO

VIA XXV

9

10

V. PENISOLA

7

VIA DELLA CHIUSA

VIA CAPPUCCINI

1

GRAND HOTEL DEI CASTELLI

5

VIA FOSSI

FREE BEACH

13

(Private)

ROMANESQUE CHURCH

RUINED CHAPEL

Baia del Silenzio

N

Ligurian Sea

To Punta Manara

200 Meters

200 Yards

Eateries & Other

6 L'Osteria Mattana
7 Polpo Mario & Ristorante La Mainolla
8 Pelagica
9 Ice Cream's Angels
10 Bacciolo Gelato
11 Tama Gelati e Molto di Più
12 Supermarket
13 To Laundrette

Accommodations

1 Hotel Helvetia & Citta Beach Bar
2 Hotel Celeste
3 Hotel Genova
4 Albergo Marina
5 Villa Jolanda

SIGHTS IN SESTRI LEVANTE

Stroll the Town

Head out from the train station and follow Via Roma until it dead ends at the leafy city park. Go left a few blocks to Corso Colombo (just past the Bermuda Bar). This main drag will take you to the TI before turning into the mostly pedestrianized Via XXV Aprile. This street, running the length of the peninsula, is lively with shops, eateries, and delightful pastel facades. When you reach Piazza Matteotti, dominated by a large white Renaissance-era church, you'll have beaches to the right (pay) and left (free). If you continue up the lane to the left of the church, you'll pass a scenic amphitheater, then the evocative arches of a ruined chapel (bombed during World War II and left as a memorial). A few minutes farther on, past a stony Romanesque church, the road winds to the right to Grand Hotel dei Castelli. The rocky, forested bluff at the end of the town's peninsula is actually the huge private backyard of this fancy hotel.

Beaches

These are named after the bays (*baie*) that they border. The less scenic, bigger beach, **Baia delle Favole,** is divided up much of the year

The Baia del Silenzio beach is ringed by bright, colorful cafés.

(May-Sept) into sections that you must pay to enter. Fees, up to €30 per day in August, generally include chairs, umbrellas, and fewer crowds. There are several small free sections: at the ends and in the middle (look for *libere* signs, and ask *"Gratis?"* to make sure that it's free). For less expensive sections of beach (where you can rent a chair for about €8-10), ask for *spiaggia libera attrezzata* (spee-AH-jah LEE-behr-ah ah-treh-ZAHT-tah). The usual beach-town activities are clustered along this *baia*: boat rentals, sailing lessons, and bocce courts.

The town's other beach, **Baia del Silenzio,** is picturesque, narrow, virtually all free, and jam-packed, providing a good chance to see Italian families at play. There isn't much more to do here than unroll a beach towel and join in. Because of the bay's small size and the currents, the water gets warmer here than at **Baia delle Favole.** At the far end of Baia del Silenzio (under recommended Hotel Helvetia) is the **$$ Citto Beach bar,** which offers front-row seats with bay views (summer until very late, spring and fall until sunset, sandwiches and salads at lunchtime only, Gilberto).

SLEEPING IN SESTRI LEVANTE

$$$$ Hotel Helvetia, overlooking Baia del Silenzio, feels posh and romantic, with 21 plush rooms, a large sun terrace with a heated, cliff-hanging swimming pool, and a peaceful garden atmosphere. With doubles renting for €400-plus in peak season, it's a big but enticing splurge (family rooms, air-con, elevator, shuttle to off-site pay parking, closed Nov-March, Via Cappuccini 43, tel. 0185-41175, www.hotelhelvetia.it, helvetia@hotelhelvetia.it, Alex).

$$$ Hotel Celeste, a dream for beach lovers, rests along the waterfront. Its 41 rooms are modern, crisp, and pricey, but you're paying for the sea breeze (family rooms, air-con, elevator, attached beachside bar/breakfast terrace, Lungomare Descalzo 14, tel. 0185-485-005, www.hotelceleste.com, info@hotelceleste.com, Franco).

$$ Hotel Genova, well-run by the Bertoni family, has 19 shiny-clean, modern, and cheery rooms (three with sea view), a sunny lounge, rooftop sundeck, free loaner bikes, and a good location just two blocks from Baia delle Favole (ask for quieter room in back, family rooms, air-con, elevator, pay parking, Viale Mazzini 126, tel. 0185-41057, www.hotelgenovasestrilevante.com, info@hotelgenovasestri levante.com, Stefano). They also book apartments in a nearby palazzo (www.appartamentisestrilevante.com).

$$ Albergo Marina's friendly Magda and her brother Santo rent 23 peaceful, clean, good-value rooms painted in sea-foam green. Though the hotel is on a busy boulevard in the more urban part of town, rooms face a quiet back courtyard and it's a short walk to the beach (family rooms, air-con, elevator, free self-service laundry, pool table, closed Nov-Easter, Via Fascie 100, tel. 0185-41527, www.marina hotel.it, marinahotel@marinahotel.it).

$ Villa Jolanda is a homey, bare-bones pensione on the hilly old-town streets beyond the pedestrian zone. It has 17 dated rooms (5 with little balconies and territorial views) and a garden courtyard/sun terrace—perfect for families on a budget (family rooms, pay parking, near Piazza Matteotti at Via Pozzetto 15—go up the lane to the right of the church, tel. 0185-41354, www.villajolanda.it, info@villajolanda.it, Mario).

EATING IN SESTRI LEVANTE

You'll find many eateries along the classic Via XXV Aprile, which also abounds with *focaccerie,* takeout pizza by the slice, and little grocery shops. Assemble a picnic or try one of the places below.

$$ L'Osteria Mattana has long, shared tables in two white-tiled dining rooms (one in front and the other past the wood oven and brazier). Daily specials—most featuring seafood—are listed on chalkboard menus (lunch Sat-Sun only 12:30-14:30, dinner daily 17:30-22:30, closed Mon Oct-April, cash only, Via XXV Aprile #34, tel. 0185-457-633, Marco).

$$$ Polpo Mario serves traditional seafood dishes and pastas from their fun people-watching location on the main drag (daily 12:00-15:00 & 19:00-23:30 except closed for lunch on Mon, Via XXV Aprile 163, tel. 0185-480-203).

$$$ Pelagica, a contemporary restaurant with a choice spot overlooking the Baia delle Favole, focuses on seafood—from anchovies to fried squid to traditional fish soup. Their rooftop terrace doubles as a cocktail lounge in the evening (daily 12:30-14:30 & 17:00-late, closed Wed in off-season, Via Pilade Queirolo 7, mobile 388-20255).

$$ Ristorante La Mainolla offers pizzas, big salads, focaccia sandwiches, and reasonably priced pastas near Piazza Matteotti (daily 12:00-16:00 & 19:00-22:00, Via XXV Aprile 187, tel. 0185-42792).

Gelato: Tourists flock to **Ice Cream's Angels,** at the intersection of Via XXV Aprile and Via della Chiusa, where Riccardo and Elena artfully load up your cone and top it with a dollop of Nutella chocolate-hazelnut cream (open daily until late in summer). **Bacciolo** enjoys a similar popularity (closed Thu, Via XXV Aprile 51, on the right just before the church). **Tama Gelati e Molto di Più** makes their gelato daily with fresh ingredients (near the beach at Baia delle Favole, Viale Rimembranza 34).

SESTRI LEVANTE CONNECTIONS

By **train,** Sestri Levante is 30 minutes from Monterosso (hourly connections with Monterosso; nearly hourly with other Cinque Terre towns, requiring a change in Levanto or Monterosso) and 30 minutes from Santa Margherita Ligure (2/hour).

Boats depart to the Cinque Terre, Porto Venere, Santa Margherita Ligure, Portofino, and San Fruttuoso from the dock (molo) on the peninsula (Easter-Oct, tel. 0185-284-670, www.traghettiportofino.it).

Santa Margherita Ligure

If you need the Riviera of movie stars, park your yacht at Portofino. Or you can settle down with more elbow room in nearby and more personable Santa Margherita Ligure (SAHN-tah mar-geh-REE-tah lee-GOO-reh), one hour by train from the Cinque Terre. On a quick day trip to Santa Margherita Ligure from the Cinque Terre, walk the beach promenade and see the old town center before catching the bus or boat to Portofino to discover what all the fuss is about. With more time, Santa Margherita Ligure (pop. 10,200) makes a fine overnight stop or a home base for a foray into the Cinque Terre.

Santa Margherita Ligure spills down the hill to its sunny waterfront promenade.

ORIENTATION TO
SANTA MARGHERITA LIGURE

Santa Margherita Ligure tumbles easily downhill from its train station. The town has a fun Old World resort character and a breezy harborfront with a beach promenade. With its nice big-city vitality, it feels bustling and lived-in, even off-season.

Tourist Information: The TI is as central as can be, in a green kiosk at the harborside of the city traffic hub, Piazza Vittorio Veneto (daily 9:30-13:00 & 16:30-19:00, shorter hours off-season, tel. 0185-205-456, www.smlturismo.it). The ATP bus office has a ticket desk there, and bus #82 to Portofino stops at the curb in front.

Arrival in Santa Margherita Ligure

By Train: The station is a pleasant, low-stress scene. The bar/café (facing track 1) stores bags (small fee) and sells bus, train, and sightseeing-boat tickets.

To get from the station to the city center, take the stairs marked *Mare* (sea) down to the harbor; or turn right and head more gently down Via Roma, which leads to the town center, the TI, the start of my town walk, and recommended hotels (about 10 minutes away on foot). Bus #82 to Portofino stops a few steps below the station (4/hour, buy €3 one-way or €5 round-trip ticket at station bar/café, €1 more from driver).

By Car: Ask your hotelier about parking; some have free spots. Otherwise, try a private pay lot such as the Garage Europa *autopark* next to the post office (Via Roma 38). An hourly pay-and-display lot is by the harbor, in front of the fish market. Parking is generally free where there are white lines; blue lines mean you pay.

HELPFUL HINTS

Market: A market sets up on Fridays on Corso Matteotti (8:00-13:00).

Laundry: Self-service **Bolle Blu** is near Piazza Mazzini (daily 7:00-22:30, Via Roccatagliata 39, mobile 335-642-7203).

Bike Rental: Ciclomania rents city and ebikes by the day and can put together guided day trips to nearby destinations (Mon-Sat 8:30-12:00 & 15:30-19:00, closed Sun, Via Luigi Bozzo 22, tel. 0185-283-530, www.ciclomania-liguria.it, Mimmo).

Scooter Rental: GM Rent rents scooters and Smart Cars (daily 10:00-13:00 & 16:30-20:00, Via XXV Aprile 11, tel. 0185-284-420, www.gmrent.it, Francesco).

Taxi: Taxis wait outside the train station and charge €15 for a ride anywhere in town, €25 to Paraggi beach, and €35 to Portofino (tel. 0185-286-508).

Driver: Helpful taxi driver **Alessandro** has cars and minivans, and offers airport transfers to Genoa, Milan, Florence, and Nice. He also does local excursions, including day trips to the Cinque Terre (mobile 338-860-2349, www.alessandrotaxi.com, alessandrotaxi@yahoo.it).

SANTA MARGHERITA LIGURE WALK

Get your bearings with this self-guided walk, starting on Piazza Caprera, the square facing the exuberant Baroque facade of the Basilica of Santa Margherita.

Basilica of Santa Margherita

The town's main church is textbook Italian Baroque (free, daily 7:30-12:00 & 15:00-18:30). Its 18th-century facade hides a 17th-century interior slathered with art and dripping with chandeliers. The altar is typical of 17th-century Ligurian altars—shaped like a boat, with lots of shelf space for candles, flowers, and relics. Its centerpiece is a much-venerated statue of Our Lady of the Rose that's adorned this altar since 1756.

Baroque is theater...and this altar is stagecraft. After the Vatican II decrees of the 1960s, priests began to face their flocks instead of the

The town has pedestrian-friendly squares...

...and an impressive church.

Santa Margherita Ligure

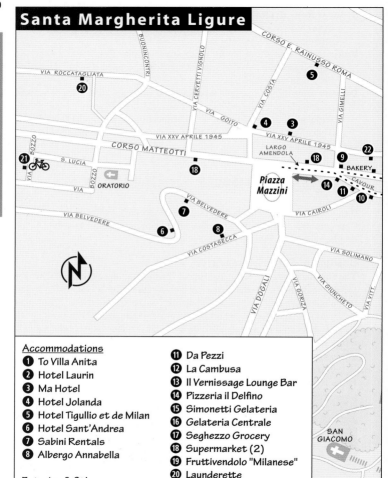

Accommodations
1. To Villa Anita
2. Hotel Laurin
3. Ma Hotel
4. Hotel Jolanda
5. Hotel Tigullio et de Milan
6. Hotel Sant'Andrea
7. Sabini Rentals
8. Albergo Annabella

Eateries & Other
9. Angolo 48
10. Vineria Machiavello
11. Da Pezzi
12. La Cambusa
13. Il Vernissage Lounge Bar
14. Pizzeria il Delfino
15. Simonetti Gelateria
16. Gelateria Centrale
17. Seghezzo Grocery
18. Supermarket (2)
19. Fruttivendolo "Milanese"
20. Launderette
21. Bike Rental
22. Scooter Rental

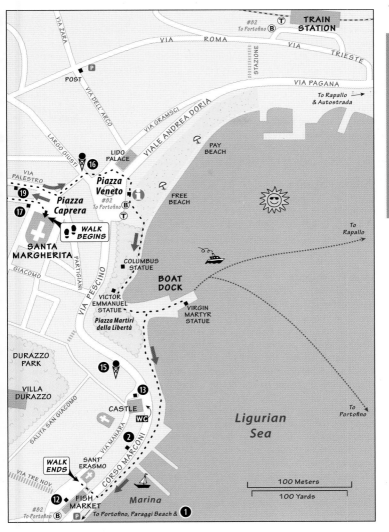

VIA ZARA

TRAIN STATION

#82 To Portofino B T

VIA ROMA

VIA TRIESTE

VIA STAZIONE

P
POST

VIA PAGANA

VIA DELL'ARCO

To Rapallo & Autostrada

VIA GRAMSCI

VIALE ANDREA DORIA

PAY BEACH

LARGO GIUSTI

LIDO PALACE

VIA PALESTRO

19

16

Piazza Veneto

FREE BEACH

17

Piazza Caprera

#82 To Portofino B T

WALK BEGINS

SANTA MARGHERITA

COLUMBUS STATUE

BOAT DOCK

To Rapallo

GIACOMO

VIA PESCINO

PARTIGIANI

VICTOR EMMANUEL STATUE

Piazza Martiri della Libertà

VIRGIN MARTYR STATUE

DURAZZO PARK

15

To Portofino

VILLA DURAZZO

13

SALITA SAN GIACOMO

CASTLE

WC

Ligurian Sea

VIA MANARA

2

CORSO MARCONI

WALK ENDS

SANT' ERASMO

VIA TRE NOV.

100 Meters

100 Yards

12

FISH MARKET

Marina

1

#82 To Portofino B

P

To Portofino, Paraggi Beach &

old altars. For this reason, all over the Catholic world, modern tables serving as post-Vatican II altars stand in front of earlier altars, like the one here, that are no longer the center of attention during Mass.

Wander the church and its chapels, noticing the inlaid-marble floors and sparkling glass chandeliers. As you marvel at the richness, remember that the region's aristocrats amassed wealth from trade from the 11th to the 15th century. When Constantinople fell to the Turks in 1453, free trade in the Mediterranean stopped, and Genovese traders became bankers—making even more money. A popular saying of the day was, "Silver is born in America, lives in Spain, and dies in Genoa." Bankers here served Spain's 17th-century royalty and aristocracy, and their accrued wealth paid for the art you see here.

Piazza Caprera

Each day this square hosts a few farmers selling their produce. On the corner of Via Cavour, just next to the basilica, visit **Seghezzo,** a venerable grocer where locals know they'll find whatever they need.

▶ *Now side-trip up the "via principale" (main drag) of the city, Via Palestro/Via Cavour. You'll go two blocks up to Piazza Mazzini and back.*

"Via Principale"

The main "street" here is really two parallel streets divided by very tall, narrow buildings. As you head up Via Cavour (on the left, by Seghezzo grocery) check out the shops on the right: The buildings that separate Via Cavour from Via Palestro are so skinny you see right through to the other side. The mix of fine boutiques, wine bars, jewelers, and casual restaurants hints at the elite—but not flashy—ambience of the town.

In two blocks, you'll emerge onto a square, Piazza Mazzini, with enough elbow room to study the pastel house fronts. These facades were painted and decorated in the characteristic Ligurian trompe-l'oeil style from the turn of the last century. Every building presents some sort of illusion—the decorators went so far as to add painted-on upper windows, shutters, and window frames.

Now do a U-turn onto Via Palestro to return to where we started (staying straight past the recommended **Angolo 48** restaurant on the corner). Walking here, notice that you're surrounded by Italians doing the same *passeggiata.* At #34 (on the left), you'll pass a traditional **panificio** (bakery) where you can say, *"Vorrei un etto di focaccia"* to treat yourself to about a quarter-pound of the region's famed bread. Just beyond, on the right at #13, **Fruttivendolo "Milanese"** is just one of the many greengrocers in town selling an array of tempting produce and glass-jarred delicacies.

▶ *Back on Piazza Caprera, turn left and walk away from the church one block to busy Largo Antonio Giusti. Across the street, a penguin marks a recommended gelateria. Head right to Piazza Vittorio Veneto, with its busy roundabout and little park on the harbor, where you'll find the TI, ATP bus office, and a bus stop for Portofino. Use the crosswalks to reach the promenade.*

Beachfront Promenade

Take a look to the left, along Viale Andrea Doria. The sidewalk is wider than the street, an indication that for more than 100 years this has been *the* place to promenade under century-old pastel facades. Notice the grand old **Lido Palace Hotel** with its view balconies overlooking a crowded beach scene.

Now turn right and walk into the waterfront park. At the midpoint of the park is a Christopher Columbus statue. He was born "Cristoforo Colombo" in 1451 in Genoa, near here, and first sailed on Genovese boats along this Ligurian coast. Next comes a statue of King Victor Emmanuel II, always ready to brandish his sword and create Italy.

▶ *Head out on the little pier with the white statue facing out to sea.*

View from the Pier

From here, standing with the "Santa Margherita Virgin Martyr" statue, you can take in all of Santa Margherita Ligure—from the villas dotting the hills, to the castle built in the 16th century to defend against pirates, to the exclusive hotels. Tourist boats to Portofino, the Cinque Terre, and beyond depart from this pier.

▶ *Continue along the waterfront on Corso Marconi.*

Harbor and Fish Market

On the right, notice the trendy, recommended **Il Vernissage Lounge Bar** with tables up at the base of the castle (with WCs down below). Continuing around the corner from the castle (closed to visitors), walk along the harbor. The region's largest fishing fleet—20 boats—ties up here. The fishing industry survives, drag-netting octopus, shrimp, and miscellaneous "blue fish." The **fish market** (Mercato del Pesca, across the street, inside the rust-colored building with arches and columns) wiggles weekdays from about 16:00 until 20:00 or so—depending on who's catching what and when. It's a cool scene as fishermen take bins of freshly caught fish directly to waiting customers.

▶ *Climb the narrow brick stairs just to the right of the fish market to a delightful little square. Find the characteristic, black-and-white pebble mosaic and relax on the benches to enjoy harbor views. Facing the square is the little...*

Oratory of Sant'Erasmo

Named for St. Erasmus, the protector of sailors, this building is an "oratory" where a brotherhood of faithful men who did anonymous good deeds congregated and worshipped. While rarely open, do check. The interior is decorated with ships and paintings of storms that local seafarers survived—thanks to St. Erasmus. The huge crosses standing in the nave are carried through town on special religious holidays.

▶ *Our walk is over. For a little extra exercise to see a pleasant park, climb the long stairs from here up to the Church of San Giacomo (with an interior similar to the Basilica of Santa Margherita) and Durazzo Park.*

SIGHTS IN SANTA MARGHERITA LIGURE

Durazzo Park (Parco di Villa Durazzo)

This park is a delight, with a breezy café, a carefully coiffed Italian garden, and an intentionally wild "English garden" below (free, daily 9:00-19:00, July-Aug until 20:00, closes earlier off-season, WC near café). The Italian garden is famous for its varied collection of palm trees and an extensive collection of camellias. It's OK to feed the large turtles in the central pond (they like bits of fish or meat).

The park is dominated by **Villa Durazzo.** It's not worth touring for most, but its remarkable pebble courtyard, carpeted in a fleur-de-lis pattern of white and gray stone, is worth a look.

Beaches (*Spiagge*)

The handiest free beaches are just below the train station toward the boat dock (see map). But the best beaches are on the road to Portofino, including my favorite, **Giò e Rino** (just before Covo di Nord Est),

Enjoying a sunny day on one of Santa Margherita Ligure's beaches.

which has sunbeds for rent and a fun, youthful crowd. The beach on the south side of **Grand Hotel Miramare** offers a more relaxing experience and is good for kids. Also nice is **Minaglia,** with rentable sunbeds and kayaks. These beaches are a 20-minute walk from downtown, or you can take bus #82 from the train station or from in front of the TI at Piazza Veneto.

Paraggi, a small, sandy beach halfway to Portofino (and an easy stop on the bus #82 route), is better than any of the close-in Santa Margherita Ligure beaches, but it's pricey (as much as €60/day in July and Aug)—and it can be packed with sun worshippers from Portofino (where there's no beach—only rocks). There's more than one *bagni* establishment here, so choose the one that most appeals. Off-season, the entire beach is all yours and free. A narrow patch of sand smack-dab in the middle of Paraggi beach is free year-round.

SLEEPING IN SANTA MARGHERITA LIGURE

$$$$ **Villa Anita** is an elegant-yet-homey family hotel run by Daniela and her son, Sandro. They rent 12 tidy rooms—nearly all with terraces—overlooking a peaceful residential neighborhood a five-minute

uphill walk from the seaside boulevard. The in-house chef offers a varying menu of Ligurian specialties nightly (dinner extra, family rooms, playground, small gym, small heated pool and sauna, loaner bikes, air-con, free parking, closed in winter, Viale Minerva 25, tel. 0185-286-543, www.hotelvillaanita.com, info@hotelvillaanita.com).

$$$$ Hotel Laurin, nestled up against castle ruins, offers 44 slick, modern, and pricey rooms looking onto the sea. All double rooms face the harbor and have terraces; on the rooftop sundeck, there's a small pool and gym. Enrico and staff are helpful (RS%, double-paned windows, elevator, air-con, limited pay parking—request when you reserve, just past the castle at Corso Marconi 3, tel. 0185-289-971, www.laurinhotel.it, info@laurinhotel.it).

$$$ Ma Hotel is a crystal-chandelier-classy boutique hotel with a fresh, modern flair. Although it sits along a busy street, its 11 stylish and spacious rooms are at the back of the building (air-con, patio, free minibar, loaner bikes, Via XXV Aprile 18, tel. 0185-280-224, www.ma hotel.it, info@mahotel.it, Annalisa).

$$$ Pastine Hotels is a chain of three well-run hotels that combines solid service, sumptuous public spaces, and pleasant rooms. The two main branches are around the corner from each other, an easy walk from the station: **Hotel Jolanda** has lavish public spaces and regal colors, and its 50 pleasant rooms have a soothing decor (RS%, air-con, elevator, free use of small weight room, pay dry sauna, free loaner bikes, Via Luisito Costa 6, tel. 0185-287-512, www.hoteljolanda.it, info@hoteljolanda.it); **Hotel Tigullio** et de Milan is smaller and tidier, with updated rooms. The superior rooms are especially nice, but even most standard doubles come with a terrace—specify when you book. The rooftop sun terrace offers sunbeds, a bar, and hot tub in the summer (RS%, air-con, elevator, free loaner bikes, pay parking, Via Rainusso 3, tel. 0185-287-455, www.hoteltigullio.eu, info@hotel tigullio.eu). The newest branch, the boutique-like **Hotel Sant'Andrea,** has 11 rooms just above Piazza Mazzini, with a patio and whirlpool for guests (RS%, air-con, pay parking, Via Belvedere 10, tel. 0185-293-487, www.hotelsantandrea.net, info@hotelsantandrea.net).

$$ Sabini Rentals, in a dull but central residential zone, offers three straightforward rooms and one apartment with a tiny corner kitchen (RS%, family rooms, 2-night minimum, cash only, breakfast on request, laundry service, Via Belvedere 31, mobile 338-902-7582, www.sabinirentals.com, info@sabinirentals.com, Cristina and Giancarlo).

$ Albergo Annabella is an old-style budget throwback with 11 rooms—some basic but most renovated. The more expensive rooms with bathrooms and air-conditioning are overpriced, but the cheaper rooms with shared bath and fans are a solid budget option (family rooms, no breakfast, air-con, Via Costasecca 10, tel. 0185-286-531, info@albergoannabella.it, Annabella speaks just enough English).

EATING IN SANTA MARGHERITA LIGURE

In the City Center

$$$ Angolo 48, run by savvy Elisa and Valentina, serves well-presented and reasonably priced Genovese and Ligurian dishes. This cozy locale is popular: Either arrive right when they open or make a reservation. There's great seating both on the square and inside. Try their handmade *pansotti* in walnut sauce (lunch Sat-Sun only 12:00-13:45, dinner Tue-Sun 18:30-22:00, closed Mon, Via Palestro 48, tel. 0185-286-650).

$$ Vineria Machiavello feels more urban Tuscan than seaside Ligurian. This well-stocked *enoteca* (wine shop) offers tastings and full bottles, but also serves a short menu of well-priced dishes, including beef and salmon tartare, at a few humble tables tucked between the wine racks (Wed-Mon 10:00-14:00 & 17:30-24:00, closed Tue, in the heart of the pedestrian zone at Via Cavour 17, tel. 0185-286-122).

$$ Da Pezzi, with a cheap cafeteria-style atmosphere, is packed with locals at midday and at night. They're standing at the bar munching *farinata* (crêpes made from chickpeas, available Oct-May 18:00-20:00), or enjoying pesto and fresh fish in the dining room. Consider the deli counter with its Genovese picnic ingredients (Sun-Fri 10:00-14:00 & 18:15-21:00, table service after 12:00 and 18:00, closed Sat, Via Cavour 21, tel. 0185-285-303, Giancarlo and Giobatta).

On the Waterfront

All along the harbor side of Via Tommaso Bottaro, south of the marina, you'll find restaurants, pizzerias, and bars serving food with a nautical view.

$$$ La Cambusa, perched above the fish market, is popular for its seafood. While the food is forgettable, the view from its harborside terrace is not. In cooler weather, the terrace is covered and heated.

Diners receive a free glass of *sciacchetrà* (dessert wine) and biscotti with this book (daily 12:00-15:00 & 19:00-23:00 except closed Thu Oct-June, Via Tommaso Bottaro 1, tel. 0185-287-410, www.ristorante lacambusa.net).

At **$$ Il Vernissage Lounge Bar,** you can nurse your drink with a million-dollar view appreciated by tourists and locals alike. There are 20 wines by the glass, plus cocktails and *spritzes,* which come with a nice plate of finger food (daily 18:00-late, Sun from 11:00, Salita al Castello 8, mobile 349-220-5846, Sandro).

Budget Options

$$ Pizzeria il Delfino, which serves thin, big, wood-fired pizzas, offers a rustic, fun local scene, with a few quiet tables outside and tight inside seating under nautical bric-a-brac (cash only, daily 12:00-15:00 & 18:00-23:00 except closed Tue dinner, Via Cavour 29, tel. 0185-286-488).

Gelato: The best *gelateria* I've found in town—with chocolate-truffle *tartufato*—is **Simonetti** (under the castle at Piazza Martiri della Libertà 48). **Gelateria Centrale,** just off Piazza Veneto near the cinema, serves up *pinguino* (penguin), a cone with your choice of gelato dipped in chocolate (Largo Antonio Giusti 14).

Groceries: Classy **Seghezzo** is a well-stocked grocery, deli, and wine shop, and great for a meal to go—ask them to *riscaldare* (heat up) their white *lasagne al pesto* or dish up their special *carpaccio di polpo*—thinly sliced octopus (Thu-Tue 7:30-13:00 & 15:30-20:00, closed Wed, near the church on Via Cavour, tel. 0185-287-172). Cheaper and less romantic, the **Carrefour Express** (Largo Amendola 5) and **Co-op** grocery (Corso Giacomo Matteotti 9) are good places to stock up on well-priced Ligurian olive oil, pasta, and pesto (both generally open daily 8:00-21:00).

SANTA MARGHERITA LIGURE CONNECTIONS

To reach the **Cinque Terre** towns (beyond Monterosso), you'll usually have to change in Sestri Levante, Levanto, or Monterosso.

From Santa Margherita Ligure by Train to: Sestri Levante (2/hour, 30 minutes), **Monterosso** (hourly, 45 minutes), **La Spezia** (hourly, 1-1.5 hours), **Pisa** (1-2/hour, 2 hours, most with transfer, less frequent InterCity/IC goes direct), **Florence** (8/day, 4 hours, transfer in Pisa), **Milan** (about hourly, 2.5 hours, more with transfer in Genoa), **Ventimiglia**/French border (4/day, 4 hours; or hourly with change in Genoa), **Venice** (at least hourly, 6 hours with changes).

By Boat to the Cinque Terre: Tour boats make various trips to Vernazza, Porto Venere, and other ports nearly every day. Pick up a schedule of departures and excursion options from the TI, visit the ticket shack on the dock, call 0185-284-670, or check www.traghetti portofino.it.

Portofino

Santa Margherita Ligure, with its aristocratic architecture, hints at old money. But nearby Portofino (pop. 500)—with its sleek jewelry shops, art galleries, and haute couture boutiques filling a humble village shell—has the sheen of new money. It's the kind of place where the sailing masts are taller than the houses and church steeples. But the *piccolo* harbor, classic Italian architecture, and wooded peninsula turn glitzy Portofino into an appealing destination. Just a couple of miles down the coast, it's a fun, easy day trip from Santa Margherita Ligure.

Planning Your Time: In summer, my favorite Portofino plan is to visit in the late afternoon. Leave Santa Margherita Ligure by bus at about 16:30, get off at Paraggi beach, and hike 30 minutes over the bluff into Portofino. Explore the town, splurge for a drink on the harborfront, or get a takeout fruity sundae (*paciugo;* pah-CHOO-goh) and sit by the water. Then return by bus to Santa Margherita Ligure for dinner (confirm late departures). If you plan to do some hiking around Portofino, come earlier in the day.

Tourist Information: The TI is tucked under an arch between the harbor and the bus stop (Wed-Mon 10:00-13:00 & 14:00-18:00, closed Tue, Via Roma 35, tel. 0185-269-024, www.comune.portofino. genova.it).

Popular with celebrities, Portofino is a classic Riviera beach town: pricey and pretty.

GETTING TO PORTOFINO

You can reach Portofino from Santa Margherita Ligure by bus or boat, or on foot. For a fun combination, you could go one way by bus and on foot from Paraggi, and the other way by boat. (I wouldn't suggest biking it, because of the blind corners.)

By Bus: Catch bus #82 from Santa Margherita Ligure's train station or at bus stops along the harbor (main stop in front of TI, €3 one-way or €5 round-trip, €1 more if bought from driver, 4/hour, 20 minutes, goes to Paraggi beach and then to Portofino). Buy tickets at the train station bar, the green ticket machine outside the TI, or any newsstand, tobacco shop, or shop that displays a *Biglietti Bus* sign. If you're at the Piazza Veneto TI kiosk, grab a bus schedule to plan your return (last bus around 24:00 in summer).

By Boat and Bus: If you're arriving in Portofino by boat, but will be busing back, follow the narrow lanes up from the harbor to the bus stop in Piazza della Libertà (ticket machine and tobacco store there sell tickets).

By Taxi: A taxi ride from Santa Margherita Ligure costs around €35 to Portofino or €25 to Paraggi beach (more at night). Taxi stands

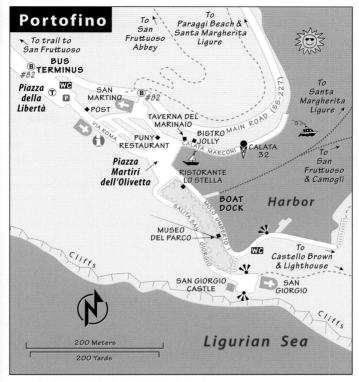

Portofino

To trail to San Fruttuoso

To San Fruttuoso Abbey

To Paraggi Beach & Santa Margherita Ligure

BUS TERMINUS #82

Piazza della Libertà

WC

SAN MARTINO

#82

POST

VIA ROMA

MAIN ROAD (SS-227)

To Santa Margherita Ligure

TAVERNA DEL MARINAIO

BISTRO JOLLY

PUNY RESTAURANT

CALATA MARCONI

CALATA 32

To San Fruttuoso & Camogli

Piazza Martiri dell'Olivetta

RISTORANTE LO STELLA

BOAT DOCK

Harbor

Cliffs

MUSEO DEL PARCO

SALITA SAN GIORGIO

MOLO UMBERTO

WC

To Castello Brown & Lighthouse

SAN GIORGIO CASTLE

SAN GIORGIO

200 Meters

200 Yards

Ligurian Sea

Cliffs

in Santa Margherita Ligure are at the train station and at the curb in front of the TI.

By Boat: The boat makes the 15-minute trip with more class and scenery, and without the traffic jams. The dock in Santa Margherita Ligure juts out from the waterfront park at Piazza Martiri della Libertà, near the TI (€7 one-way, €12 round-trip; hourly departures May-Oct daily 9:15-15:15, fewer off-season; purchase tickets at the dock or onboard, tel. 0185-284-670, www.traghettiportofino.it).

On Foot: To hike from Santa Margherita Ligure to Portofino, you have two options: You can follow the sidewalk along (and sometimes hanging over) the sea (1 hour, 2.5 miles)—although traffic can be noisy, and in places, the footpath disappears. Or, if you're hardy and ambitious, you can take a quieter two-hour hike by leaving Santa Margherita Ligure at Via Maragliano, then follow the Ligurian-symbol trail markers (keep a close eye out for red-and-white stripes). This hike takes you high into the hills. Keep left after Cappelletta delle Gave. Several blocks past a castle, you'll drop down into Paraggi beach, where you'll take the Portofino trail the rest of the way.

Bus-and-Hike Option: For a shorter—but rewarding—30-minute hike into Portofino, ride bus #82 from Santa Margherita Ligure only as far as Paraggi beach (tell the driver you want to get off there—you can't miss the inlet bay with a sandy beach). At the Portofino end of the beach, look for the *Parco di Portofino* sign to find the steps that begin the hilly, paved trail marked *Pedonale per Portofino* high above the road. There's a fair amount of up and down, but it's all well-paved and scenic. After Paraggi, you'll curl around another bay—with the famously top-end Hotel Splendido hovering on the hill above—before snaking your way to Portofino.

SIGHTS IN PORTOFINO

▲▲ Self-Guided Visual Tour from the Harbor

Stand or sit on the angled boat launch where Piazza Martiri dell'Olivetta meets the harbor (or nurse an overpriced cocktail at the nearby café tables), and get oriented to Portofino. It's one of the Mediterranean's most beautiful and famous little resorts.

Scanning the narrow pastel houses around the harbor, notice the painted-on details—as in Santa Margherita Ligure. You may also see laundry hanging out to dry—a surprising reminder that, while Ferragamo and Prada may reside on street level, actual villagers still live upstairs.

Now look out to the well-protected natural harbor—which has held substantial strategic value ever since the Romans first founded a town here. Since then, it has been appreciated by everyone from Napoleon to the Nazis.

A new flock of fans arrived in the 1950s, when *National Geographic* ran a beautiful article on the idyllic port. Locals claim that's when the Hollywood elite took note. Liz Taylor and Richard Burton came here annually (as did Liz Taylor and Eddie Fisher). During one famous party, Rex Harrison dropped his Oscar into the bay (it was recovered). Ava Gardner came down from her villa each evening for a drink—sporting her famous fur coat. Greta Garbo loved to swim naked in the harbor, not knowing (or caring) that half the town was watching. Truman Capote also called Portofino home. But VIPs were also here a century earlier. Friedrich Nietzsche famously wrote about philosophizing with the mythical prophet Zarathustra on the path between Portofino and Santa Margherita Ligure.

Today, the celebrity cachet lives on. When you tell locals you're going to Portofino, they say, "Maybe you'll see George and Amal Clooney!" Count the yachts and the tall-masted sailboats, and imagine who might be on them.

Now scan the panorama on the hillside in front of you. On the left is **Castello Brown,** an actual medieval castle built by the Genovese in the 16th century to protect this strategic harbor. It later became a private mansion, and today is a museum featuring lush gardens, sweeping viewpoints, and exhibits about Portofino and its history (€5, daily 10:00-18:00, June-Aug until 19:00, shorter hours off-season, tel. 0185-267-101, www.castellobrown.com).

Panning right, you'll see the **Church and Castle of San Giorgio,** with its popular two-way viewpoint terrace, looking down over the port and out over the ocean. This is an easy option for a picnic with grand views. Boats back to Portofino depart from the harborfront below this church. The Museo del Parco (described next) is also along this embankment.

Now look back toward town. A tidy grid of narrow cobbled streets angles gently uphill to the modern part of town, around Piazza della Libertà (with bus stop and taxi stand). These streets—where budget takeaway eateries and grocery stores are mixed in with swanky shops—are a good place to hunt for picnic fare. Up on the right is the striped church of San Martino, marking the well-manicured, enjoyable 30-minute trail to Paraggi beach.

Museo del Parco

For an artsy break, walk around the harbor to the right, where you can stroll around a park littered with 148 contemporary sculptures by mostly Italian artists, including a few top names (€5, open Wed-Mon

Portofino's harborfront

Stop for a dip at Paraggi beach.

10:00-13:30 & 15:00-20:00 in summer; closed Tue, off-season, and in bad weather).

Hikes

The TIs in Portofino and Santa Margherita Ligure can outline your options. For even more detail, the **Parco di Portofino** can provide information on the many hiking trails that crisscross Portofino's regional parklands (in Santa Margherita Ligure at Viale Rainusso 1, tel. 0185 289-479, www.parcoportofino.it). Here are two options easily accessible from Portofino.

Lighthouse Hike: A paved stone path winds up and down to the lighthouse (*faro*) at the scenic point beyond the Church and Castle of San Giorgio. Start your climb on little Salita San Giorgio—it's tucked between the Delfino and Tripoli restaurants on the harborfront. Spend a few minutes enjoying the views on the church terrace (and if it's open, duck into the cemetery with a view behind the church). Rejoin the path signed *al Faro* to continue up. Walls and hedges block views at some points, but in the end, you'll be rewarded with the open sea—and a lounge/bar (open May-Sept, 25-minute walk). Consider popping into the medieval Castello Brown on the way up or down.

Paraggi Beach Hike: You can stroll the hilly pedestrian promenade through the trees from Portofino to Paraggi beach, and, if you're lucky, see a wild boar en route (30 minutes, path starts to the right of striped Divo Martino church just above the harborfront piazza, and ends at ritzy Paraggi beach, where bus #82 stops on its way back to Santa Margherita Ligure—though in peak season, the bus may be full and won't stop).

Portofino offers all kinds of harborside dining, but the quality often doesn't match the high prices. I'd rather dine in Santa Margherita Ligure. But if you do eat in Portofino, **$$$ Ristorante lo Stella,** just a few steps from the boat dock, has well-prepared dishes, friendly servers, and portholes in the bathrooms (tel. 0185-269-007). **$$$ Taverna del Marinaio,** across the harbor, has a prime location (soaking up the last of the day's sun), tables under arcades, and a small, cozy, classy interior (tel. 0185-269-103); next door, **$$$ Bistro Jolly** offers high prices at marine-varnished tables with comfy nautical cushions. And **$$$$ Puny,** at the top of the harborfront square, is a famous splurge (reserve ahead, tel. 0185-269-037).

For budget options, you'll find a variety of *foccacerie,* pizzerias, and grocery stores hiding out in the tiny grid of streets just up from the water. For dessert, opposite the boat dock, walk out to the little **Calata 32** *gelateria.*

South of the Cinque Terre

South of the Cinque Terre is the nothing-special town of La Spezia, a handy transit hub with excellent train connections. But nearby is a gem—the resort town of Porto Venere, worthy of a day trip by boat from the Cinque Terre or by bus from La Spezia.

Porto Venere

The perfect antidote to gritty La Spezia hides just around the bay: the enchanting resort of Porto Venere (POR-toh VEH-neh-reh). Comparably scenic to the Cinque Terre towns—but with a bit of glitz—this village clings to a rocky, fortress-crowned promontory. A rainbow of tall, skinny pastel facades rises up from an inviting harborfront promenade.

Porto Venere is light on sights, but it's a breeze to reach by boat from the Cinque Terre and fun to explore: The higher you go, the better the views. Rather than the open sea, Porto Venere faces the beautiful Gulf of La Spezia—more romantically known as the Gulf of Poets—where Lord Byron was said to have gone for a hardy swim despite rough seas and local warnings to the contrary. (He survived... at least, for a little while longer.) Scanning the bay, you'll see the outskirts of muscular La Spezia, the often-snow-covered peaks of the Apuan Alps, the resort town of Lerici, and—across a narrow strait—the rugged island of Palmaria.

ORIENTATION TO PORTO VENERE

Tourist Information: The TI fills an old guard tower at the top of the main square (daily 10:00-12:00 & 15:00-19:00, closed Wed off-season, Piazza Bastreri 7, tel. 0187-790-691, www.prolocoportovenere.it).

   Getting There: Porto Venere is an easy day trip from the Cinque Terre towns by **boat** (late April-mid-Oct, 1.5 hours from Monterosso, €23 one-way, €35 day pass includes hopping on and off, operated by 5 Terre-Golfo dei Poeti, tel. 0187-732-987, see schedule at www.navigazionegolfodeipoeti.it). You can also cruise between Porto Venere and Santa Margherita Ligure, with stops in Vernazza and

Lovely Porto Venere offers grand views to hikers and a harborfront promenade.

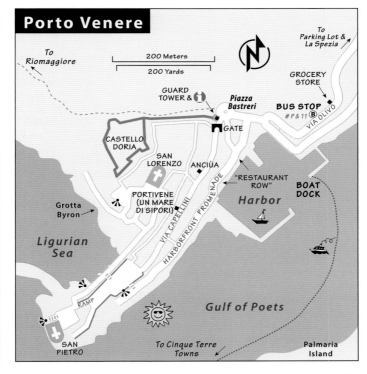

Porto Venere

To Riomaggiore

To Parking Lot & La Spezia

200 Meters
200 Yards

N

GUARD TOWER & ℹ

Piazza Bastreri

GROCERY STORE

BUS STOP
#P & 11 Ⓑ
VIA OLIVO

GATE

CASTELLO DORIA

SAN LORENZO

ANCIÙA

"RESTAURANT ROW"

BOAT DOCK

PORTIVENE (UN MARE DI SIPORI)

VIA CAPELLINI

HARBORFRONT PROMENADE

Harbor

Grotta Byron

Ligurian Sea

RAMP

Gulf of Poets

SAN PIETRO

To Cinque Terre Towns

Palmaria Island

Sestri Levante, using a different boat line (www.traghettiportofino.it). The scenic **bus** ride between La Spezia and Porto Venere curls around the Gulf of Poets (see the end of the chapter).

For **drivers,** parking is challenging. In peak season, shuttle buses connect the parking lot just outside Porto Venere to the harborside square. Otherwise, test your luck with the pay spots on the seaside.

Visiting Porto Venere

The town is essentially two streets deep: the harborfront promenade and, a block uphill, the main street (Via Capellini). A complete loop around Porto Venere includes both of these streets and a moderately steep hike up to the town's two main churches and fortress for the views. You can see everything in just a few hours; add more time for lunch or lingering.

Along the **harborfront,** seafood restaurants enjoy a Technicolor backdrop, and boat captains try to talk you into a 40-minute excursion around three nearby islands. But the real town lives on **Via Capellini** (just through the big arch from the TI—or hike up any of the narrow stepped lanes from the harbor). Skinny and shaded, Via Capellini has a mix of restaurants, focaccia-and-pizza takeaway stands, several local shops, and boutiques selling gourmet gifty edibles and gaudy beachwear.

At the west end of the promenade and Via Capellini, the town comes to a point at the late-13th-century **Church of San Pietro,** with Gothic features and a black-and-white-striped interior typical of this region. Climb the stairs to the roof terrace for fine views in both directions (including the "Grotta Byron" sea cave).

More viewpoints line the walk from here up the stairs to the town's other big church, **San Lorenzo.** With a dark and brooding Romanesque interior, this church—like much of Porto Venere—was

Porto Venere's narrow lanes offer a mix of shops and restaurants.

built by the Genovese to establish a strategic foothold at the entrance to the bay in the 12th century.

From in front of the church, more steps lead up to the town's fortress, **Castello Doria.** A hulking shell, it's not worth the money to go inside, but a hike up to the terrace out front is rewarded with striking panoramas.

From the castle, head back into town; to make this walk a loop, bear left to follow the very steeply stepped lane that runs just inside the crenellated wall back down to the TI.

Hardy **hikers** enjoy the five-hour (or more) hike to Riomaggiore, the nearest Cinque Terre town. For more on hiking the Cinque Terre, see page 20.

EATING IN PORTO VENERE

On the harbor, next to colorful bobbing boats, take your pick of views and menus (seafood/pizza) for a meal in a memorable setting.

For better values and more variety, stroll one block inland to Via Capellini. For a sit-down meal along here, try **$$ Portivene (Un Mare di Sipori),** serving local dishes with modern flair at reasonable prices (reservations smart, closed Mon, at #94, tel. 0187-792-722). Better yet, browse the fun selection of takeaway shops (selling pizza slices, bruschetta, focaccia, and top-notch deli items) to put together a picnic to enjoy by the port. **$ Anciùa** (at #40) assembles *panini* to order with interesting ingredients; they also have fresh fried anchovies and other Ligurian street food.

La Spezia

While just a quick train ride south of the fanciful Cinque Terre (15-30 minutes), the working city of La Spezia (lah SPEH-tsee-ah; pop. 94,000) feels like "reality Italy." Primarily a transit point connecting to the Cinque Terre, lovely Porto Venere, or to Pisa, Lucca, and other Tuscan towns, La Spezia is slim on sights and has no beaches. The city is also the entry point for big cruise ships funneling groups into the Cinque Terre.

Arrival in La Spezia: The La Spezia Centrale **train** station has various services lined up along track 1. In the middle of the platform you'll find a city **TI** (daily 9:00-18:00, tel. 0187-026-152, www.myspezia.it) and a Cinque Terre **National Park information desk,** where you can buy park tickets—including the Cinque Terre Treno Card that includes both trains and trails (daily 7:30-19:30, shorter hours off-season, tel. 0187-743-500, www.parconazionale5terre.it). Don't use the more remote La Spezia Migliarina station, where some trains terminate.

For **drivers** who want to leave a car in La Spezia, then head to the Cinque Terre by train, the easiest parking is under the train station, at the modern Park Centro Stazione (enter from Via Fiume or Via Paleocapa, €26/day, www.mobpark.eu). Free parking is at Piazza d'Armi, a 20-minute walk or short bus ride from the station (entrance at Via XV Giugno 1918).

Visiting La Spezia

If you find yourself with extra time here, and would like a meal, a museum stop, or a stroll, here's how to accomplish all three: Exit the station, turn left, and walk a long downhill block (on Via Paleocapa Pietro) to the roundabout at Piazza Saint Bon, which marks the start of a pleasant pedestrian zone—with several eateries—on **Via Fiume** (which turns into **Via del Prione**). Continuing on this street to the harborfront gardens makes a nice stroll (it's one mile from station to harbor). Along the way, you'll pass the nearly deserted **Museo Amedeo Lia,** which displays Italian paintings from the 13th to 18th century, including minor works by Venetian masters Titian, Tintoretto, and Canaletto (€10, Tue-Sun 10:00-18:00, closed Mon, tel. 0187-731-100, http://museolia.spezianet.it).

Near La Spezia: Without a doubt, the most appealing sight is outside La Spezia: **Porto Venere.** This gorgeous Cinque Terre-esque town, overlooking a beautiful bay, is just a 30-minute bus ride away (described earlier in this chapter).

La Spezia

400 Meters
400 Yards

To Il Gelsomino
To Cinque Terre & Genoa
TRAIN STATION
CINQUE TERRE PARK OFFICE

VIA FIUME
V. A. FERRARI
V. LAMARMORA

Piazza Brin

VIA FIRENZE
V. TORINO
CORSO V. MILANO NAPOLI
VIA CAVOUR
V. ROMANO
V. V. BIXIO

Piazza S. Bon.

RAIL TUNNEL

To Pisa

BAG STORAGE

SPALLANZANI TUNNEL

VIA DEL COLLI
V. XXVI MARZO
V. DEL PRIONE

CRISTO RE CATHEDRAL

VIALE G. AMENDOLA

VIA GAETA
VIA GRAMSCI

VIALE GARIBALDI

VIA MONALE
VIA MILLE
VIA ROSSELLI

MUSEO AMEDEO LIA

Piazza Cavour

To Train Station & Porto Venere

Piazza Europa

To A12 Autostrada

POST
V. FAZIO
V. CHIODO

V. BART.

CORSO CAVOUR
VIA MAGENTA
V. DEL PRIONE

PHARMACY

CRUISE TERMINAL

PIAZZA D'ARMI

To Porto Venere & Cinque Terre

NAVAL AREA (PRIVATE)

Lagora Canal

VIALE G. AMENDOLA

V. V. SETT.
VIA GRAMSCI
V. MAZZINI
VIALE ITALIA WATERFRONT PROMENADE

Piazza Chiodo

Harbor

NAVAL MUSEUM

Boats to Lerici, Porto Venere & Cinque Terre

To

VIA CRISPI
VIA VENETO

Accommodations
1. Hotel Firenze e Continentale
2. Via Chiodo Luxury Rooms
3. Casa Danè (2)
4. L'Arca di Noè B&B

Eateries & Other
5. Locanda del Mercato & Avis Car Rental
6. La Pia Centenaria

7. Ristorante Roma
8. To Mirabello Gourmet
9. Antica Trattoria Sevieri
10. All'Inferno dal 1905
11. Covered Market
12. Launderette
13. Piazza d'Armi (Free Parking)
14. Porto Venere Bus Stop

SLEEPING IN LA SPEZIA

Stay in the Cinque Terre if you can, but if you're in a bind, these accommodations are within a 10-minute walk of the station. Most include breakfast: **$$$ Hotel Firenze e Continentale** is your grand, Old World splurge (68 rooms, RS%, air-con, elevator, pay parking garage, Via Paleocapa 7, tel. 0187-713-200 or 0187-713-210, www.hotelfirenze continentale.it, info@hotelfirenzecontinentale.it).

$$ Via Chiodo Luxury Rooms, with nine elegant, bright white rooms, is a soothing retreat close to the public gardens (air-con, elevator, pay parking, Via Chiodo 13, tel. 0187-22-607, www.costaestate.it, info@costaestate.it). They also rent an apartment in Porto Venere.

For *affittacamere* rooms for rent, consider the stylish **$$ Casa Danè,** offering 10 chic rooms with comfy linens and orange trees outside the door, plus 20 more rooms inside the train station (some rooms overlook the tracks but good windows reduce the noise, family rooms, air-con, Via Paleocapa 4, mobile 347-351-3239, www.casadane.it, reception@casadane.it, Paolo). The homey **$ L'Arca di Noè B&B** has three bright, artsy, affordable rooms, all with private bath (air-con, comfy communal kitchen, Via Fiume 39, mobile 320-485-2434, monti alessandra@email.it, Alessandra).

$ Il Gelsomino, best for drivers, is a homey and tranquil, three-room B&B in the hills above La Spezia overlooking the Gulf of Poets (family rooms, reconfirm arrival time in advance, Via dei Viseggi 9, tel. 0187-704-201, www.ilgelsomino.biz, ilgelsomino@inwind.it, gracious Carla and Walter Massi).

EATING IN LA SPEZIA

These eateries are located between the train station and the harbor.

$$ Locanda del Mercato offers Ligurian specialties that you can savor inside or out. For a food adventure, try the risotto with pumpkin cream or the roasted octopus (Tue-Sun 12:00-15:00 & 19:00-23:00, closed Mon, Via Fratelli Rosselli 88, tel. 0187-732-651).

$ La Pia Centenaria hosts local crowds at its counters at all hours of the day for its specialty—*farinata* (a chickpea pancake that can be eaten plain or with savory toppings). You can also get pizza (Mon-Sat 10:00-22:00, closed Sun, Via Magenta 12, tel. 0187-739-999).

$$$ Ristorante Roma, next to the train station, is open long hours. Their reasonable fixed-price meals even include wine, and several dishes are flavored with truffles (daily 6:00-23:30, Via Pietro Paleocapa 18, tel. 0187-189-0177).

$$ Mirabello Gourmet serves light, delicious meals from a fun, informal location at the Mirabello Marina (Tue-Wed 10:00-15:00, Thu-Sun 8:00-15:00 & 18:00-23:00, closed Mon, Porto Mirabello, Viale Italia, tel. 0187-174-0168).

$$$ Antica Trattoria Sevieri is an elegant place close to the Piazza del Mercato, featuring fresh fish, seafood pastas, and risotto (Mon-Sat 12:00-15:00 & 19:00-24:00, closed Sun, Via della Canonica 13, tel. 0187-751-1776).

$ All'Inferno dal 1905 is a small, busy restaurant with a laid-back atmosphere, serving traditional chickpea soup, linguine with mussels, and homemade pesto (Mon-Sat 12:15-14:30 & 19:30-22:30, closed Sun, tel. 0187-29458, Via L. Costa 3).

LA SPEZIA CONNECTIONS

Trains leave about twice hourly for the **Cinque Terre towns** (direction: Levanto). A few express trains (headed to Genoa or Milano) stop only at Monterosso. Other connections from La Spezia include **Pisa** (about hourly, 1 hour), **Florence** (5/day direct, 2.5 hours, otherwise nearly hourly with change in Pisa), **Rome** (8/day direct, more with transfers in Pisa, 3-4 hours), **Milan** (about hourly, 3 hours direct or with change in Genoa), and **Venice** (about hourly, 5-6 hours, 1-3 changes).

It's also possible to go by **boat** to the Cinque Terre, Porto Venere, and outer islands from the La Spezia dock (www.navigazionegolfo deipoeti.it).

City **buses to Porto Venere** generally depart from Viale Garibaldi; the bus stop is about a 10-minute walk from the train station (see the "La Spezia" map; bus #P, 2/hour, 30 minutes, €3 each way; also bus #11 mid-June-mid-Sept, sporadically off-season; confirm schedule and buy tickets at TI; tickets also sold at tobacco shops, bars, and newsstands).

Practicalities

HELPFUL HINTS

Travel Tips

Hurdling the Language Barrier: Many Italians—especially those in the tourist trade and in big cities—speak English. Still, you'll get better treatment if you learn and use Italian pleasantries. Italians have an endearing habit of talking to you even if they know you don't speak their language—and yet, thanks to gestures and thoughtfully simplified words, it somehow works. Don't stop them to tell them you don't understand every word—just go along for the ride. For a list of survival phrases, see page 177.

Time Zones: Italy, like most of continental Europe, is generally six/nine hours ahead of the East/West Coasts of the US. For a handy time converter, use the world clock app on your phone or download one (see www.timeanddate.com).

Business Hours: Most businesses are open Monday through Saturday, generally 9:00 to 13:00 and from 15:30-16:00 to 19:00-19:30, Monday through Saturday. Many shops stay open through lunch or later into the evening, especially larger stores in tourist areas. Shops in small towns and villages are more likely to close during lunch. Stores are usually closed on Sunday, and often on Monday.

Watt's Up? Europe's electrical system is 220 volts, instead of North America's 110 volts. Most electronics (laptops, smartphones, cameras) and new hair dryers convert automatically, so you won't need a converter, but you will need an adapter plug with two round prongs, sold inexpensively at travel stores in the US. Sockets in Italy only accept plugs with slimmer prongs: Don't buy an adapter with the thicker ("Schuko" style) prongs.

Learning some Italian will endear you to locals.

Use an ATM attached to a bank for lower fees.

PRACTICALITIES

Helpful Websites

Tourist Information: For all of Italy, see www.italia.it. For the Cinque Terre: www.cinqueterre.it; for Cinque Terre National Park: www.parconazionale5terre.it.
Passports and Red Tape: www.travel.state.gov
Cheap Flights: www.kayak.com (for international flights), www.skyscanner.com (for flights within Europe)
Airplane Carry-on Restrictions: www.tsa.gov
European Train Schedules: www.bahn.com
General Travel Tips: www.ricksteves.com (helpful info on train travel, rail passes, car rental, using your mobile device, travel insurance, packing lists, and much more—plus updates to this book)

Safety and Emergencies

Emergency and Medical Help: For any emergency service—ambulance, police, or fire—call **112** from a mobile phone or landline. Operators, who generally speak English, will deal with your request or route you to the right emergency service. If you get sick, do as the locals do and go to a pharmacist for advice. Or ask at your hotel for help—they'll know the nearest medical and emergency services.

Theft or Loss: Petty theft is common in heavily touristed sights. With sweet-talking con artists meeting you at the station and pickpockets dressed as tourists, travelers face a gauntlet of rip-offs. Pickpockets troll tourist crowds around major sights and at train stations. They don't want to hurt you—they usually just want your money and gadgets. Green or sloppy tourists are prone to scams. Thieves strike when you're distracted. Don't trust overly kind strangers. Keep nothing important in your pockets, and be especially careful with expensive mobile phones.

To replace a **passport,** you'll need to go in person to an embassy or consulate. **US** embassy in Rome—tel. 06-46741 for 24-hour emergency line, tel. 06-4674-2420 for nonemergencies, by appointment only (Via Vittorio Veneto 121). Consulates in Milan—tel. 02-290-351 (Via Principe Amedeo 2/10) and Florence—tel. 055-266-951 (Lungarno Vespucci 38). For all, see http://it.usembassy.gov. **Canadian** embassy in Rome—tel. 06-854-441 (Via Zara 30); Milan—tel. 02-626-94238 (Piazza Cavour 3). For both, see www.italy.gc.ca.

If you lose your **credit** or **debit card,** report the loss immediately. With a mobile phone, call these 24-hour US numbers: Visa (tel. +1 303/967-1096), MasterCard (tel. +1 636/722-7111), and American Express (tel. +1 336/393-1111). From a landline, you can call these US numbers collect by going through a local operator. For more information, see www.ricksteves.com/help.

MONEY

Italy uses the euro currency: 1 euro (€) = about $1.20. To convert prices in euros to dollars, add about 20 percent: €20 = about $24, €50 = about $60. (Check www.oanda.com for the latest exchange rates.)

Here's my basic strategy for using money in Italy: Upon arrival, head for a cash machine (ATM, called a *bancomat*) and withdraw some local currency, using a debit card with low international transaction fees. Keep your cards and cash safe in a money belt.

Although credit cards are widely accepted in Europe, cash is sometimes the only way to pay for cheap food, bus fare, taxis, tips, and local guides. Some businesses (especially smaller ones, such as B&Bs and mom-and-pop cafés and shops) may charge you extra for using a credit card—or might not accept credit cards at all. Having cash on hand helps you out of a jam if your card randomly doesn't work.

US credit cards generally work fine in Europe. Some European card readers will accept your card as-is while others may generate a receipt for you to sign or prompt you to enter your PIN (so it's important to know the code for each of your cards).

At self-service payment machines (transit-ticket kiosks, parking, etc.), results are mixed, as US cards may not work in some unattended transactions. If your card won't work, look for a cashier who can process your card manually—or pay in cash.

Shopping, VAT Refunds, and Customs

The Cinque Terre has limited options for shoppers, such as tacky (if fun) beach trinkets and T-shirts. Some of the towns have higher-quality art boutiques. But in general, the Cinque Terre's best souvenirs are edible: a jar of pesto; dried *trofie* pasta to go with it; olive oil; the sweet *sciacchetrà* dessert wine; and lemon-flavored or -scented goods

Tipping

Tipping in Italy isn't as automatic and generous as it is in the US.

Restaurants: In Italy, a service charge *(servizio)* is usually built into your check (look at the bill carefully). If it is included, there's no need to leave an extra tip. If it's not included, it's common to leave about €1 per person (a bit more at finer restaurants) or to round up the bill.

Taxis: For a typical ride, round up your fare a bit (for instance, if the fare is €4.50, pay €5).

Services: In general, if someone in the tourism or service industry does a super job for you, a small tip of a euro or two is appropriate...but not required.

(since Liguria is one of just two places in Italy with serious lemon production).

Getting a VAT Refund: If you spend more than €155 on goods at a single store, you may be eligible to get a refund of the 22 percent Value-Added Tax (VAT). Have the store fill out the paperwork; you'll need to show them your passport. At the airport, get your papers stamped by customs before going through security, then process your refund through a service such as Global Blue or Planet (for details, see www.ricksteves.com/vat).

Customs for American Shoppers: You're allowed to take home $800 worth of items and one liter of alcohol per person duty-free. You can take home many processed and packaged foods (e.g., vacuum-packed cheeses, chocolate) but not fresh produce or most meats. Any liquid-containing foods must be packed (carefully) in checked luggage. To check customs rules and duty rates, visit http://help.cbp.gov.

SLEEPING

Accommodations in the popular Cinque Terre cost more than in other villages and are packed on holidays (especially Easter weekend and April 25); when the weather is best (May, June, Sept, and Oct); and on Fridays and Saturdays all summer (though July and Aug can be less crowded due to sweltering heat). During these busy periods, you must reserve ahead.

Sleep Code

Dollar signs reflect average rates for a standard double room with breakfast in high season.

$$$$	**Splurge:** Most rooms over €170
$$$	**Pricier:** €130-170
$$	**Moderate:** €90-130
$	**Budget:** €50-90
¢	**Backpacker:** Under €50
RS%	**Rick Steves discount**

Unless otherwise noted, credit cards are accepted, hotel staff speak basic English, and free Wi-Fi is available. If the listing includes RS%, request a Rick Steves discount.

Vernazza, the spindly and salty essence of the Cinque Terre, is my top choice for a home base. And its summer opera series has beefed up its nightlife. But if you think too many people have my book, you'll get fewer crowds and better value for your money in other towns.

Monterosso is a good choice for sun-worshipping beach lovers, those who prefer the ease of a real hotel, and a youthful crowd interested in nightlife.

Manarola, charming and not overrun, draws serious hikers and sophisticated Europeans. The town has a good range of professional-feeling small accommodations, but fewer dining and evening options.

Riomaggiore, one of the biggest Cinque Terre towns, has the cheapest beds and rivals Monterosso for nightlife, but it's more Italian than Rivieran.

Corniglia, on a hilltop (no beach), attracts hermits, anarchists, wine lovers, and mountain goats.

Private Rooms for Rent (*Affittacamere*): Many accommodations in the Cinque Terre (especially in Vernazza) are *affittacamere,* or private rooms for rent. These range from simple bedrooms with shared baths, to fancy bedrooms with private baths, to comfortable apartments (often with small kitchens). You get a key and come and go as you like, typically rarely seeing your landlord. Plan on paying cash. If you must cancel an *affittacamere* reservation, do it as early as

possible—since people renting rooms usually don't take deposits, they lose money if you don't show up.

Amenities: Breakfast is not included at most *affittacamere* and other simple accommodations. (Locals take breakfast about as seriously as flossing.) The basic, very Italian choice is simply to drop by a neighborhood bar for a cappuccino and a *cornetto* (croissant) or a piece of focaccia. Some pricier places include breakfast, but this often consists of a few paltry items (packaged croissants, yogurt, instant coffee) in a minifridge in your room.

While air-conditioning is essential in the summer elsewhere in Italy, in the breezy Cinque Terre you can generally manage fine without it. Expect thin walls (pack earplugs).

Near the Cinque Terre

Riviera towns typically have modern hotels with the usual amenities. The hotels aren't necessarily cheaper than the Cinque Terre, but they are more likely to have space. High season is July and August; prices go down in April-June and September-October, and are soft the rest of the year. Some hotels close off-season. Especially in peak season, some hoteliers want you to pay for half-pension (lunch or dinner).

EATING

Hanging out at a seaview restaurant while sampling local specialties could become one of your favorite Cinque Terre memories.

The key staple is anchovies (*acciughe;* ah-CHOO-gay)—ideally served the day they're caught. If you've always hated anchovies (the slimy, salty kind), try them fresh here. They're prepared in a dizzying variety of ways: marinated, salted, drenched in lemon juice, butterflied

PRACTICALITIES

Events in the Cinque Terre

You could use this list to find and join a festival—or to avoid crowds. For more festival information and to confirm dates, check www.lamia liguria.it. Food festivals in particular are subject to change.

Easter and Easter Monday	**Popular time to visit the Cinque Terre.** As it's extremely crowded, book long in advance.
April 25	**Italian Liberation Day** is also very crowded (avoid this day, as locals literally shut down the trails).
May 1	**Labor Day** (Cinque Terre packed with day-trippers)
May (3rd Sunday)	**Monterosso: Lemon Festival**
June (3rd Sunday)	**Monterosso: Anchovy Festival**
June 23	**Monterosso and Vernazza: Feast of Corpus Domini** (procession on carpet of flowers)
June 24	**Riomaggiore and Monterosso: Feast day of St. John the Baptist** (procession and fireworks, floating candles on the sea; big fire on Monterosso's old-town beach the day before)
June 29	**Corniglia: Feast day of Sts. Peter and Paul**
July 20	**Vernazza: Feast day of patron St. Margaret,** with fireworks
Aug (1st Sunday)	**Vernazza: Feast of Nostra Signora di Reggio** (hike up to Madonna di Reggio sanctuary for food and church procession)
Aug 10	**Manarola: Feast day of patron St. Lawrence**
Aug 15	**Feast of the Assumption** (Ferragosto)
Sept 8	**Monterosso:** Feast of Madonna di Fegina (luminarias and procession up to hilltop sanctuary)

Restaurant Price Code

Dollar signs reflect the cost of a typical main course.

$$$$ **Splurge:** Most main courses over €20
$$$ **Pricier:** €15-20
$$ **Moderate:** €10-15
$ **Budget:** Under €10

Pizza by the slice and other takeaway food is **$**; a basic trattoria or sit-down pizzeria is **$$**; a casual but more upscale restaurant is **$$$**; and a swanky splurge is **$$$$**.

and deep-fried (sometimes with a tasty garlic/vinegar sauce called *giada*), and so on.

Tegame alla vernazzana is the most typical main course in Vernazza: a layered, casserole-like dish of whole anchovies, potatoes, tomatoes, white wine, oil, and herbs.

Seafood is plentiful. You'll often see *muscoli ripieni* (stuffed mussels) on menus. And, while antipasto means cheese and salami in Tuscany, here you'll get *antipasti frutti di mare* (or simply *antipasti misti*): a plate of mixed "fruits of the sea." Many restaurants are proud of their *frutti di mare*—it's how they show off—and it's a fine way to start a meal. For two diners, splitting one of these and a pasta dish can be plenty.

This region is the birthplace of pesto. Basil, which loves the temperate Ligurian climate, is ground with cheese (half *parmigiano* and half pecorino), garlic, olive oil, and pine nuts, and then poured over pasta. You'll see it on gnocchi or on pasta designed specifically for pesto to cling to: *trenette* (ruffled on one side) or *trofie* (short, dense twists). Many also like pesto lasagna, made with white sauce.

Pansotti are ravioli with ricotta and a mixture of greens, often served with a walnut sauce (*salsa di noci*)...delightful and filling.

Focaccia—pillowy, flat, salty, olive-oily bread—also originates here in Liguria. The baker roughs up the dough with finger holes, sprinkles it with salt water, then bakes it. Focaccia comes plain or with onions, sage, or olives, and is a local favorite for a snack on the beach. Bakeries sell it in rounds or slices by weight (a portion is about 100 grams, or *un etto*).

Farinata, a humble flatbread snack sold at pizza and focaccia places, is made from chickpea flour, water, oil, and pepper and baked on a copper tray in a wood-burning stove. It's dense, filling, and less flavorful than focaccia.

The region also loves its locally grown lemons. The popular lemon liqueur is called *limoncino* (a.k.a. *limoncello*).

Vino delle Cinque Terre, while not one of Italy's top wines, flows cheap and easy throughout the region. It's white—crisp, refreshing, and great with seafood. Local wines are typically blends, predominantly using the bosco grape, found only here. As local wine has become more sophisticated and appreciated lately, there are now plenty of wine bars that offer tasting experiences.

For a sweet but potent dessert wine, *sciacchetrà* (shah-keh-TRAH) is worth a try (18 percent alcohol, often served with dunkable cookies). While 10 kilos of grapes yield 7 liters of local wine, *sciacchetrà* is made from near-raisins: 10 kilos make only 1.5 liters of the wine. The word means "push and pull"—push in lots of grapes, pull out the best wine.

STAYING CONNECTED

Making International Calls

For the dialing instructions below, use the complete phone number, including the area code (if there is one).

From a Mobile Phone: It's easy to dial with a mobile phone. Whether calling from the US to Europe, country to country within Europe, or from Europe to the US—it's all the same: Press zero until you get a + sign, enter the country code (39 for Italy), then dial the phone number.

From a US Landline to Europe: Dial 011 (US/Canada access code), country code (39 for Italy), and phone number.

From a European Landline to the US or Europe: Dial 00 (Europe access code), country code (1 for the US), and phone number.

To make a collect call to the US, contact the local operator. It's generally not possible to dial Italian toll or toll-free numbers from a US mobile or landline (although you can sometimes get through using Skype). For more phoning help, see www.howtocallabroad.com.

Budget Tips for Using a Mobile Phone in Europe

Sign up for an international plan. To stay connected at a lower cost, sign up for an international service plan through your carrier. Most providers offer a simple bundle that includes calling, messaging, and data.

Use free Wi-Fi whenever possible. Unless you have an un-limited-data plan, you're best off saving most of your online tasks for Wi-Fi. Most accommodations in Europe offer free Wi-Fi, and many cafés have free hotspots for customers. You'll also often find Wi-Fi at TIs, city squares, major museums, public-transit hubs, airports, and aboard trains and buses.

Minimize the use of your cellular network. Even with an international data plan, wait until you're on Wi-Fi to Skype, download apps, stream videos, or do other megabyte-greedy tasks. Using a navigation app such as Google Maps over a cellular network can take lots of data, so do this sparingly or offline.

Use Wi-Fi calling and messaging apps. Skype, WhatsApp, FaceTime, and Google Hangouts are great for making free or low-cost calls or sending texts over Wi-Fi worldwide.

RESOURCES FROM RICK STEVES

Begin your trip at RickSteves.com: This guidebook is just one of many titles in my series on European travel. I also produce a public television series, *Rick Steves' Europe,* and a public radio show, *Travel with Rick Steves.* My mobile-friendly website is *the* place to explore Europe in preparation for your trip. You'll find thousands of fun articles, videos, and radio interviews; a wealth of money-saving tips; travel news dispatches; a video library of my travel talks; my travel blog; my latest guidebook updates (www.ricksteves.com/update); and my free Rick Steves Audio Europe app. You can also follow me on Facebook, Instagram, and Twitter.

Packing Checklist

Clothing

- ❑ 5 shirts: long- & short-sleeve
- ❑ 2 pairs pants (or skirts/capris)
- ❑ 1 pair shorts
- ❑ 5 pairs underwear & socks
- ❑ 1 pair walking shoes
- ❑ Sweater or warm layer
- ❑ Rainproof jacket with hood
- ❑ Tie, scarf, belt, and/or hat
- ❑ Swimsuit
- ❑ Sleepwear/loungewear

Money

- ❑ Debit card(s)
- ❑ Credit card(s)
- ❑ Hard cash (US $100-200)
- ❑ Money belt

Documents

- ❑ Passport
- ❑ Tickets & confirmations: flights, hotels, trains, rail pass, car rental, sight entries
- ❑ Driver's license
- ❑ Student ID, hostel card, etc.
- ❑ Photocopies of important documents
- ❑ Insurance details
- ❑ Guidebooks & maps
- ❑ Notepad & pen
- ❑ Journal

Toiletries Kit

- ❑ Soap, shampoo, toothbrush, toothpaste, floss, deodorant, sunscreen, brush/comb, etc.
- ❑ Medicines & vitamins
- ❑ First-aid kit
- ❑ Glasses/contacts/sunglasses
- ❑ Sewing kit
- ❑ Packet of tissues (for WC)
- ❑ Earplugs

Electronics

- ❑ Mobile phone
- ❑ Camera & related gear
- ❑ Tablet/ebook reader/laptop
- ❑ Headphones/earbuds
- ❑ Chargers & batteries
- ❑ Plug adapters

Miscellaneous

- ❑ Daypack
- ❑ Sealable plastic baggies
- ❑ Laundry supplies
- ❑ Small umbrella
- ❑ Travel alarm/watch

Optional Extras

- ❑ Second pair of shoes
- ❑ Travel hairdryer
- ❑ Water bottle
- ❑ Fold-up tote bag
- ❑ Small flashlight & binoculars
- ❑ Small towel or washcloth
- ❑ Tiny lock
- ❑ Extra passport photos

Italian Survival Phrases

Hello. (informal)	Ciao.	**chow**
Good day.	Buongiorno.	bwohn **jor**-noh
Do you speak English?	Parla inglese?	**par**-lah een-**gleh**-zay
Yes. / No.	Sì. / No.	see / noh
I (don't) understand.	(Non) capisco.	(nohn) kah-**pees**-koh
Please.	Per favore.	pehr fah-**voh**-ray
Thank you.	Grazie.	**graht**-see-ay
Excuse me.	Mi scusi.	mee **skoo**-zee
Goodbye.	Arrivederci.	ah-ree-veh-**dehr**-chee
one / two / three	uno / due / tre	**oo**-noh / **doo**-ay / tray
How much does it cost?	Quanto costa?	**kwahn**-toh **koh**-stah
I'd like / We'd like...	Vorrei / Vorremmo...	voh-**reh**-ee / voh-**reh**-moh
...a room.	...una camera.	**oo**-nah **kah**-meh-rah
...a ticket.	...un biglietto.	oon beel-**yeh**-toh
...a bike.	...una bicicletta.	**oo**-nah bee-chee-**kleh**-tah
Where is...?	Dov'è...?	doh-**veh**
...the station	...la stazione	lah staht-see-**oh**-nay
...tourist information	..informazioni per turisti	een-for-maht-see-**oh**-nee pehr too-**ree**-stee
...the toilet?	...la toilette	lah twah-**leh**-tay
men / women	uomini, signori / donne, signore	**woh**-mee-nee, seen-**yoh**-ree / **doh**-nay, seen-**yoh**-ray
left / right	sinistra / destra	see-**nee**-strah / **deh**-strah
straight	sempre dritto	**sehm**-pray **dree**-toh
What time does this open / close?	A che ora apre / chiude?	ah kay **oh**-rah ah-**pray** /**kee**-**oo**-day
now / soon / later	adesso / presto / tardi	ah-**deh**-soh / **preh**-stoh / **tar**-dee
today / tomorrow	oggi / domani	**oh**-jee / doh-**mah**-nee

In the Restaurant

I'd like / We'd like...	Vorrei / Vorremmo... voh-**reh**-ee / voh-reh-moh
...to reserve a table for one / two.	...prenotare un tavolo per uno / due. preh-noh-**tah**-ray oon **tah**-voh-loh pehr **oo**-noh / **doo**-ay
...the menu (in English).	...Il menù (in inglese). eel meh-**noo** (een een-**gleh**-zay)
service (not) included	servizio (non) incluso sehr-**veet**-see-oh (nohn) een-**kloo**-zoh
to go	da portar via dah **por**-tar **vee**-ah
with / without	con / senza kohn / **sehnt**-sah
and / or	e / o ay / oh
menu (of the day)	menù (del giorno) meh-**noo** (dehl **jor**-noh)
speciality of the house	specialità della casa speh-chah-lee-**tah** deh-lah **kah**-zah
bread / cheese	pane / formaggio **pah**-nay / for-**mah**-joh
sandwich	panino pah-**nee**-noh
soup / salad	zuppa / insalata **tsoo**-pah / een-sah-**lah**-tah
meat / poultry / fish	carne / pollo / pesce **kar**-nay / **poh**-loh / **peh**-shay
seafood	frutti di mare **froo**-tee dee mah-ray
fruit / vegetables	frutta / legumi **froo**-tah / lay-**goo**-mee
dessert	dolce **dohl**-chay
coffee / tea / water	caffè / tè / acqua kah-**feh** / teh / **ah**-kwah
wine / beer	vino / birra **vee**-noh / bee-rah
red / white	rosso / bianco **roh**-soh / bee-**ahn**-koh
glass / bottle	bicchiere / bottiglia bee-kee-**eh**-ray / boh-**teel**-yah
Cheers!	Cin cin! cheen cheen
The bill, please.	Il conto, per favore. eel **kohn**-toh pehr fah-**voh**-ray
Delicious!	Delizioso! day-leet-see-**oh**-zoh

For more user-friendly Italian phrases, check out *Rick Steves Italian Phrase Book & Dictionary*.

INDEX

Start your trip at

Our website enhances this book and turns

Explore Europe

At ricksteves.com you can browse through thousands of articles, videos, photos and radio interviews, plus find a wealth of money-saving travel tips for planning your dream trip. And with our mobile-friendly website, you can easily access all this great travel information anywhere you go.

TV Shows

Preview the places you'll visit by watching entire half-hour episodes of *Rick Steves' Europe* (choose from all 100 shows) on-demand, for free.

ricksteves.com

your travel dreams into affordable reality

Radio Interviews

Enjoy ready access to Rick's vast library of radio interviews covering travel tips and cultural insights that relate specifically to your Europe travel plans.

Travel Forums

Learn, ask, share! Our online community of savvy travelers is a great resource for first-time travelers to Europe, as well as seasoned pros.

Travel News

Subscribe to our free Travel News e-newsletter, and get monthly updates from Rick on what's happening in Europe.

Classroom Europe

Check out our free resource for educators with 400+ short video clips from the *Rick Steves' Europe* TV show.

Audio Europe™

Rick's Free Travel App

Get your FREE Rick Steves Audio Europe™ app to enjoy…

- Dozens of self-guided tours of Europe's top museums, sights and historic walks
- Hundreds of tracks filled with cultural insights and sightseeing tips from Rick's radio interviews
- All organized into handy geographic playlists
- For Apple and Android

With Rick whispering in your ear, Europe gets even better.

Find out more at ricksteves.com

Pack Light and Right

Gear up for your next adventure at rickesteves.com

Light Luggage

Pack light and right with Rick Steves' affordable, custom-designed rolling carry-on bags, backpacks, day packs and shoulder bags.

Accessories

From packing cubes to moneybelts and beyond, Rick has personally selected the travel goodies that will help your trip go smoother.

Shop at rickesteves.com

Rick Steves has

Experience maximum Europe

Save time and energy

This guidebook is your independent-travel toolkit. But for all it delivers, it's still up to you to devote the time and energy it takes to manage the preparation and logistics that are essential for a happy trip. If that's a hassle, there's a solution.

Rick Steves Tours

A Rick Steves tour takes you to Europe's most interesting places with great guides and small groups

great tours, too!

with minimum stress

of 28 or less. We follow Rick's favorite itineraries, ride in comfy buses, stay in family-run hotels, and bring you intimately close to the Europe you've traveled so far to see. Most importantly, we take away the logistical headaches so you can focus on the fun.

Join the fun

This year we'll take 33,000 free-spirited travelers—nearly half of

them repeat customers—along with us on four dozen different itineraries, from Ireland to Italy to Athens. Is a Rick Steves tour the right fit for your travel dreams? Find out at ricksteves.com, where you can also request Rick's latest tour catalog.

Europe is best experienced with happy travel partners. We hope you can join us.

See our itineraries at ricksteves.com

A Guide for Every Trip

BEST OF GUIDES

Full-color guides in an easy-to-scan format, focusing on top sights and experiences in popular destinations

Best of England
Best of Europe
Best of France
Best of Germany

Best of Ireland
Best of Italy
Best of Scotland
Best of Spain

COMPREHENSIVE GUIDES

City, country, and regional guides printed on Bible-thin paper. Packed with detailed coverage for a multi-week trip exploring iconic sights and more

Amsterdam &
  the Netherlands
Barcelona
Belgium: Bruges, Brussels,
  Antwerp & Ghent
Berlin
Budapest
Croatia & Slovenia
Eastern Europe
England
Florence & Tuscany
France
Germany
Great Britain
Greece: Athens &
  the Peloponnese
Iceland

Ireland
Istanbul
Italy
London
Paris
Portugal
Prague & the Czech Republic
Provence & the French
  Riviera
Rome
Scandinavia
Scotland
Sicily
Spain
Switzerland
Venice
Vienna, Salzburg & Tirol

Many guides are available as ebooks.

POCKET GUIDES
Compact guides for shorter city trips

Amsterdam	Italy's Cinque Terre	Prague
Athens	London	Rome
Barcelona	Munich & Salzburg	Venice
Florence	Paris	Vienna

SNAPSHOT GUIDES
Focused single-destination coverage

Basque Country: Spain & France
Copenhagen & the Best of Denmark
Dublin
Dubrovnik
Edinburgh
Hill Towns of Central Italy
Krakow, Warsaw & Gdansk
Lisbon
Loire Valley
Madrid & Toledo
Milan & the Italian Lakes District
Naples & the Amalfi Coast
Nice & the French Riviera
Normandy
Northern Ireland
Norway
Reykjavík
Rothenburg & the Rhine
Sevilla, Granada & Southern Spain
St. Petersburg, Helsinki & Tallinn
Stockholm

CRUISE PORTS GUIDES
Reference for cruise ports of call

Mediterranean Cruise Ports
Scandinavian & Northern European
  Cruise Ports

TRAVEL SKILLS & CULTURE
Greater information and insight

Europe 101
Europe Through the Back Door
Europe's Top 100 Masterpieces
European Christmas
European Easter
European Festivals
For the Love of Europe
Travel as a Political Act

PHRASE BOOKS & DICTIONARIES

French
French, Italian & German
German
Italian
Portuguese
Spanish

PLANNING MAPS

Britain, Ireland & London
Europe
France & Paris
Germany, Austria & Switzerland
Iceland
Ireland
Italy
Scotland
Spain & Portugal

PHOTO CREDITS

Avalon Travel
Hachette Book Group
1700 Fourth Street
Berkeley, CA 94710

Printed in China by RR Donnelley
First printing September 2020

ISBN: 978-1-64171-291-0

For the latest on Rick's talks, guidebooks, Europe tours, public radio show, free audio tours, and public television series, contact Rick Steves' Europe, 130 Fourth Avenue North, Edmonds, WA 98020, 425/771-8303, www.ricksteves.com, rick@ricksteves.com.

Rick Steves' Europe
Managing Editor: Jennifer Madison Davis
Assistant Managing Editor: Cathy Lu
Special Publications Manager: Risa Laib
Editors: Glenn Eriksen, Julie Fanselow, Tom Griffin, Suzanne Kotz, Rosie Leutzinger, Teresa Nemeth, Jessica Shaw, Carrie Shepherd
Editorial & Production Assistant: Megan Simms
Editorial Intern: Amelia Benich, Maxwell Eberle
Researcher: Suzanne Kotz
Graphic Content Director: Sandra Hundacker
Maps & Graphics: David C. Hoerlein, Lauren Mills, Mary Rostad
Digital Asset Coordinator: Orin Dubrow

Avalon Travel
Senior Editor and Series Manager: Madhu Prasher
Associate Managing Editors: Jamie Andrade, Sierra Machado
Copy Editor: Maggie Ryan
Proofreader: Kelly Lydick
Indexer: Claire Splan
Production & Typesetting: Christine DeLorenzo
Cover Design: Kimberly Glyder Design
Interior Design: Darren Alessi
Maps & Graphics: Kat Bennett, Mike Morgenfeld

Although the author and publisher have made every effort to provide accurate, up-to-date information, they accept no responsibility for loss, injury, cloudy days, or inconvenience sustained by any person using this book.

Let's Keep on Travelin'

Your trip doesn't need to end.

Follow Rick on social media!